MANY CULTURES,
MANY FACES
Monsignor W. Onclin Chair 2002

KATHOLIEKE UNIVERSITEIT LEUVEN
Faculteit Kerkelijk Recht
Faculty of Canon Law

MANY CULTURES, MANY FACES

Monsignor W. Onclin Chair 2002

UITGEVERIJ PEETERS
LEUVEN
2002

ISBN 90-429-1124-7
D.2002/0602/45

INHOUDSTAFEL / TABLE OF CONTENTS

DWARSVERBINDINGEN

Rik Torfs

De *Monseigneur W. Onclin Chair for Comparative Church Law*
bestaat sinds 1990. In de beginperiode werd de leerstoel op uiteen-
lopende manieren ingevuld. Het opvallendst was wellicht een colloquium over kerk en ambt dat in het Antwerpse Theologisch en Pastoraal
Centrum (TPC) van 2 tot 4 april 1992 werd georganiseerd door
mevrouw H. Warnink. Datzelfde jaar werden gastsprekers uitgenodigd,
Brian Ferme die toen nog in Oxford actief was en Frank Lyall uit Aberdeen. Later werden de studenten met lectuuropdrachten of andere vormen
van hersengymnastiek bedacht.

De *Monseigneur W. Onclin Chair* zoals die nu bestaat, kreeg gestalte
in 1995. De eerder geïmproviseerde aanpak die, met uitzondering van
het al vermelde colloquium in het TPC, tot dan toe kenschetsend was
geweest, werd verlaten. Voortaan werden elk jaar twee internationaal
vermaarde wetenschappers uitgenodigd, die elk een week lang colleges
verzorgden en aan het einde gekomen, tijdens een academische zitting,
hun gedachten lieten gaan over een onderwerp dat op dat ogenblik
hun wetenschappelijke belangstelling genoot. De lezingen werden ook
gepubliceerd.

De twee sprekers hadden, buiten hun onbetwistbare competentie, niet
noodzakelijk heel veel met elkaar gemeen. Dat gegeven is van meet af
aan duidelijk. Neem nu 1995, met monseigneur Cormac Burke, rota-
auditeur, specialist huwelijksrecht, en professor Ruud Huysmans, eerder
een expert in kerkstructuren en goed op de hoogte van het reilen en
zeilen van het instituut in onze moderne samenleving. Burke-Huysmans:
ziedaar het eerste verrassende koppeltje dat de *Monseigneur W. Onclin
Chair* opleverde. Het zou het laatste niet zijn. De latere combinaties, als-
mede de titels van hun lezingen, treft u op de slotbladzijden van dit
boekje aan: Serrano-Morrisey, Pree-Provost, Örsy-Coertzen, Migliore-
Wood, Beal-Papasthatis, Coriden-Pagé. Ongetwijfeld grote namen, maar
inmiddels: wat een diversiteit.

Die veelkleurigheid weerspiegelde zich ook in de moeilijke zoek-
tochten naar titels voor de jaarlijkse publicaties. Hadden wij maar
van meet af aan geopteerd voor een simpele nummering. *Monseigneur*

W. Onclin Chair 1, vervolgens 2 en 3 en 4, zoiets, zoals ook constructivistische schilderijen vaak netjes een cijfer kregen opgeplakt. Constructie 4. Verder geen pathos en geen poeha. Maar neen dus, wij opteerden van in den beginne voor een heuse titel, met alle gevolgen van dien: *In Diversitate Unitas* bijvoorbeeld (1997) of *Bridging Past and Future* (1998). Titels die er op wijzen dat de publicaties rondom de *Monseigneur W. Onclin Chair* geen strak gestructureerde themanummers zijn, maar een behoorlijk losse verzameling van teksten.

Over dit gebrek aan eenheid kunnen, voor liefhebbers van het genre, altijd enig obligate postmoderne opmerkingen worden geformuleerd, zoals: de brochures in het raam van de *Monseigneur W. Onclin Chair* gepubliceerd, waarschuwen door hun structuur, of liever door de afwezigheid ervan, voor een bedrieglijk harmoniemodel. Zij laten zien dat *eenheid*, zelfs in het canoniek recht, geen gegeven meer is, mogelijk wel een opgave voor wie ze als eindresultaat wenselijk acht.

Zo ongeveer zou, wat academisch en niet minder pedant, over dit gebrek aan interne eenheid, aan cohesie, bericht kunnen worden. Een dergelijke verklaring zou echter een verdraaiing van de werkelijkheid inhouden. Postmoderne doelstellingen werden bij de organisatie van de *Monseigneur W. Onclin Chair* nimmer nagestreefd. Meegaan met trends in die richting, inbegrepen klemtonen op het fragmentarische en het gesitueerde subject, mogelijk *pour les besoins de la cause* een beetje afgezwakt: dat alles was op geen enkel ogenblik een betrachting. Trouwens, misschien is het canoniek recht als wetenschapsdiscipline niet eens zo erg verbrokkeld. Daarover formuleren wij, in het raam van de Onclin Chair, geen enkele mening.

Waar wij, allemaal blijkens de recente geschiedenis van de *Monseigneur W. Onclin Chair* wel minstens impliciet in geloven, is in een veelheid van benaderingen en een overvloed aan studiemateriaal die bij een creatief omgaan met kerkelijk recht belangrijk zijn. Met name de inbreng van kerk-staat specialisten is vanaf 1995 meteen nadrukkelijk zichtbaar. Tussen de auteurs die sindsdien een bijdrage lieten verschijnen, zijn er enkele die op de eerste plaats expert zijn in de juridische verhoudingen tussen kerk en staat, zoals Ch. Papasthatis of J.E. Wood. Andere zitten zowat te paard tussen canoniek recht en kerk-staat-verhoudingen. Ook in het artikel van J. Tretera ligt de klemtoon op wat in Duitsland *Staatskirchenrecht* heet.

Kortom, de gevarieerde teksten die de oogst vormen van zeven Onclin Chairs, hebben niets te maken met enige (gemilderde) post-moderne visie over hoe kerkelijk recht functioneert of zou moeten functioneren.

Het wetenschappelijke of theologische statuut van het kerkelijk recht blijft buiten beschouwing.

De veelheid en veelkleurigheid van teksten slaat op iets geheel anders. Canoniek recht, wat zijn exacte natuur ook moge zijn, functioneert niet in een vacuüm, is geen serreplantje, is geen verheven materie die elke outsider volkomen door de vingers glipt. Integendeel, als wetenschap en als praktische discipline krijgt het kerkelijk recht gestalte via een dialoog met de omringende wereld. De juridische verhoudingen tussen kerk en staat spelen daarbij een grote, meer zelfs, een onontkomelijke rol.

Dus nogmaals, het brede spectrum waarin de teksten gepubliceerd in het raam van de *Monseigneur W. Onclin Chair* te situeren zijn, is *niet* het gevolg van een welbepaalde (fragmentarische) opvatting over canoniek recht, intern gezien dan. Neen, de veelkleurigheid slaat op de noodzakelijke openheid die het canoniek recht tegenover de buitenwereld, en eerst en vooral tegenover de juridische verhoudingen tussen kerk en staat, aan de dag dient te leggen.

Dat deze openheid op termijn consequenties kan hebben voor de identiteit van het canoniek recht, valt moeilijk te loochenen. Zoals wie reist of leest na een tijdje, onmerkbaar meestal, over bepaalde dingen anders begint te denken, zo ondergaat een open canoniek recht, op termijn, de invloed van de disciplines of impulsen waarvoor het zich openstelt. De interne gezondheidstoestand van het canoniek recht is in dat proces niet echt een bepalende factor.

Of nog, een canoniek recht dat methodologisch wat *op drift* is, trekt wellicht lering uit ontwikkelingen in het profane recht, trends in de sociologie, bewegingen in de juridische verhoudingen tussen kerk en staat. Maar dat geldt net zo goed voor een *bloeiend* kerkelijk recht, dat helemaal niet in een crisis verkeert, en dat schijnbaar aan zichzelf genoeg heeft. Ook zo'n kerkelijk recht wordt beïnvloed door allerlei dwarsverbindingen, zoals die met name met het werkveld van de verhoudingen tussen kerk en staat tot stand komen.

Op dit ogenblik van de geschiedenis bevinden wij ons kennelijk in de tweede hypothese. Het canoniek recht smacht niet naar adem, maar verkeert volgens alle officiële bronnen in een periode van hoogconjunctuur. In november 2001 werd het tienjarig bestaan van de CCEO gevierd met een groots opgezet symposium in Rome. Het recht van de kerk kreeg, in de titel van deze bijeenkomst, het ereteken *vehiculum caritatis* opgespeld. Tijdens een toespraak die hij op 22 november 2001 hield, verhaalde kardinaal Angelo Sodano hoe gelukkig paus Johannes-Paulus II met deze benaming wel was. Duidelijk moge inmiddels zijn dat een juridisch systeem waarvoor de omschrijving *vehiculum caritatis* kan worden aangewend, zich in een uitstekende gezondheid mag verheugen. Vele profane rechtsstelsels moeten het met minder doen.

En toch, ondanks dit opmonterende uitgangspunt, zijn allerlei dwarsverbindingen tussen het canonieke recht enerzijds en de juridische verhoudingen tussen kerk en staat anderzijds, duidelijk aanwijsbaar.

KERK EN STAAT OP TWEE FRONTEN

Het onvermijdelijke karakter van de kerk-staat verhoudingen, net zoals trouwens de nadrukkelijkheid waarmee zij aan de oppervlakte treden en waarmee dwarsverbindingen met het canonieke recht tot stand komen, is in het verleden niet altijd even vanzelfsprekend geweest.

Tot een eind in de twintigste eeuw werden, in Europa, de juridische verhoudingen tussen kerk en staat gekenmerkt door een sterke neiging tot *afbakening*. De regels bepaalden vooral wie bevoegd was voor welke materie. Een typisch voorbeeld is de juridische competentie met betrekking tot het huwelijk. In diverse Europese landen prijkte, in wet of grondwet, het principe dat het burgerlijk huwelijk noodzakelijk aan enige religieuze ceremonie vooraf diende te gaan[1]. Een dergelijke bepaling legt machtsverhoudingen bloot en kent bevoegdheden toe, maar laat elke *inhoudelijke* benadering van het huwelijk buiten beschouwing. Overigens bestond daar in de negentiende eeuw minder discussie over dan vandaag. Het huwelijk was een eerbiedwaardige instelling, of ze nu juridisch in handen was van de kerk dan wel door de staat werd gecontroleerd. Voor *à la carte*-verlangens van trouwlustigen was er nauwelijks ruimte. Pas later groeide het burgerlijk huwelijk geleidelijk weg van het kerkelijke, dat inmiddels in principe onontbindbaar bleef. Kortom, de juridische verhoudingen tussen kerk en staat, de bevoegdheidsafbakening met betrekking tot het huwelijk, leidde niet meteen tot dwarsverbindingen tussen de inhoud van het canonieke recht en bepaalde profaan-juridische trends.

Zo vreemd is deze vaststelling niet. De verhoudingen tussen kerk en staat vonden eertijds hun beslag op een hoog niveau, het niveau van macht en bevoegdheden. In een sfeer van competitie vonden de debatten

---

[1] In België is het principe terug te vinden in artikel 21 van de Grondwet, in Nederland in artikel 1:68 van het Burgerlijk Wetboek, in Frankrijk en in Duitsland in gewone wetgeving.

plaats. Inhoudelijke samenwerking naar aanleiding van concrete dossiers bleef zeldzaam.

Vandaag is die samenwerking er volop. En kerk en staat blijken, naast rivalen, nu ook partners te zijn, partners die geregeld allebei bij een-zelfde dossier, instituut, maatschappelijk verschijnsel betrokken zijn.

Een helder voorbeeld van deze evolutie zijn de arbeidsrelaties in de kerk, zoals het statuut van de leek die professioneel werkzaam is in het pastorale veld[2]. Zijn rechtspositie bevat doorgaans zowel een canoniek als een profaanrechtelijk facet, waarbij het evenwicht tussen beide factoren tegelijk belangrijk en delicaat is[3]. Het canoniek statuut moet de basisprincipes van het profane arbeidsrecht in rekening brengen. Het arbeidscontract, op zijn beurt, dient ruimte te scheppen voor de reli-gieuze dimensie van de werkrelatie. Of nog: het statuut van de pastoraal werker heeft iets van een *patchwork* waarin, naast canonieke elementen, ook profaanrechtelijke aspecten van belang zijn. De juridische ver-houdingen tussen kerk en staat bepalen of en in hoeverre de binnen-kerkelijke verhoudingen door de beschermingsmechanismen van het profane arbeidsrecht worden beïnvloed of gekleurd.

Die vraag kan tot bijzonder genuanceerde antwoorden leiden. Cano-niek recht en profaan recht worden niet elk op hun eigen plaats gezet, zoals dat bij de competentiestrijd met betrekking tot het huwelijk wél het geval was. Het motto is niet langer het wat kleinburgerlijke *chaque chose à sa place, et une place pour chaque chose*. Integendeel, er ont-staat ruimte voor gemengde terreinen, waarop kerk en staat elkaar ont-moeten, en beide rechtssystemen op een of andere wijze aan elkaar worden gekoppeld.

Dit soort precisiewerk komt in moderne kerk-staat-verhoudingen geregeld voor. Daarbij betrokken zijn twee systemen met een volkomen eigen inwendige dynamiek, namelijk het eerder zakelijke profane recht en zijn canonieke tegenhanger, noch min noch meer een *vehiculum cari-tatis*. Het boven aangehaalde arbeidsrecht biedt een mooi voorbeeld van deze interactie.

Een andere fraaie illustratie levert het aansprakelijkheidsrecht. In landen die in de traditie van de *Code civil* staan, is de aansteller of *commettant*

---

[2] A. BORRAS (ed.), *Des laïcs en responsabilité pastorale? Accueillir de nouveaux ministères*, Paris, Cerf, 1998, 313 p.; R. TORFS en K. MARTENS (ed.), *Parochie-assis-tenten. Leken als bedienaar van de eredienst?*, in R. TORFS (ed.), *Scripta canonica*, I, Leuven, Peeters, 1998, x + 142 p.; R. TORFS, "Les assistants paroissiaux rémunérés par l'État en Belgique", *Quaderni di diritto e politica ecclesiastica* 1998, 255-268.

[3] Niet in alle landen, in Duitsland is er meer autonomie.

aansprakelijk voor schade die onder bepaalde omstandigheden door zijn aangestelde of *préposé* wordt toegebracht. De relatie *commettant-préposé* is breder dan het loutere arbeidscontract, zoveel is zeker. Maar behelst zij ook de verhouding tussen een *bisschop* en een *pastoor*? Met andere woorden, past de canonieke relatie *bisschop-pastoor* in het profane plaatje *commettant-préposé*[4]? Onnodig aan te voeren dat een dergelijke vraagstelling een gedetailleerde analyse van beide verhoudingen vergt, met uiteindelijk een vergelijking. Een vergelijking die, gezien de eigen aard van de twee rechtssystemen, altijd een beetje mank zal lopen, maar die toch een helder antwoord behoeft, te weten ja of neen. *Ja* impliceert dat de bisschop mogelijk aansprakelijk kan worden gesteld voor bepaalde vormen van schade aan derden toegebracht door de pastoor. *Neen* betekent het omgekeerde.

Het moge duidelijk zijn dat in beide aangehaalde voorbeelden, namelijk het statuut van de pastoraal werker en het aansprakelijkheidsdossier, de dwarsverbindingen tussen het canonieke en het profane systeem zowel subtiel als delicaat zijn. De wat afstandelijke bevoegdheidsafbakening zo typisch voor de negentiende eeuw, heeft vandaag plaatsgemaakt voor een geraffineerde interactie naar aanleiding van allerlei concrete dossiers.

De toenemende *interactie* is dus een belangrijk kenmerk van hedendaagse kerk-staat-verhoudingen. Profane desiderata en technieken sijpelen op die manier langzaam het kerkelijk recht binnen, ook al is dat laatste een *vehiculum caritatis* dat het, zuiver intrinsiek gezien, uitstekend maakt en niet de behoefte voelt aan allerlei vormen van externe input. Want ook dàt is helder: het zijn de staat en het profane recht die vragende partij zijn. In een steeds meer gereguleerde maatschappij vindt de burgerlijke overheid dat sommige mechanismen die burgers bescherming bieden ook in een religieuze sfeer niet volledig afwezig kunnen blijven[5]. Anders uitgedrukt: in plaats van de negentiende-eeuwse *afba-*

---

[4] Cf. de rechtspraak dienaangaande: Corr. Brussel 9 april 1998, *Journal des tribunaux* 1998, 530, gewijzigd door Brussel 25 september 1998, *Journal des tribunaux* 1998, 712 ; Corr. Dendermonde 10 juni 1998, *Revue générale de droit civil belge* 1998, 339. Bepaalde rechtsleer meent op basis van deze enkele arresten te kunnen spreken van een gevestigde rechtspraak die deze band afwijst: zie hiervoor L.-L. CHRISTIANS, "L'autorité religieuse entre stéréotype napoléonien et exégèse canonique : l'absence de responsabilité objective de l'évêque pour son clergé en droit belge", *Quaderni di diritto e politica ecclesiastica* 2000, 951-960. Deze conclusie lijkt ons nogal voorbarig, te meer daar het Hof van Cassatie zich nog niet heeft uitgesproken over deze belangrijke rechtsvraag.

[5] R. TORFS, "The Roman Catholic Church and Secular Legal Culture in the Twentieth Century", *Studia Historiae Ecclesiasticae* 1999, 1-20.

kening, komt er nu *interactie*, maar interactie waarbij de staat aan zet is, duidelijk het initiatief neemt, dwingende normen uitvaardigt op terreinen die juridisch gezien *braakland* plachten te zijn. Braakland dat religieuze gemeenschappen toeliet resoluut een eigen koers te varen, gebaseerd op hun godsdienstig gedachtengoed.

KERK EN STAAT OP DRIE FRONTEN

De kerk zit evenwel niet altijd in het defensief. Toegegeven, zo lijkt het misschien wel even als de twee boven geschetste fasen in ogenschouw worden genomen: na een eerder evenwichtige *afbakeningsperiode* (cf. de jurisdictiestrijd m.b.t. het huwelijk) komt er een *interactieperiode* waarbij de staat eisen stelt op terreinen die voorheen juridisch braakland waren. De kerk plooit schijnbaar terug.

Schijnbaar. Want net zoals aspiraties van de staat consequenties kunnen hebben op een terrein dat voorheen exclusief canoniek was, is de omgekeerde beweging eveneens denkbaar, namelijk de beweging waarbij een kerk vanuit haar zelfverstaan weegt op de juridische verhoudingen tussen kerk en staat, en uiteindelijk zelfs op het profane recht.

Dat de omgekeerde beweging dus ook blijkt te bestaan, betekent niet, ook niet impliciet, dat kerk en staat op hetzelfde juridische niveau staat en dat derhalve de kerk als een *societas perfecta* moet worden beschouwd. Het bestaan van de omgekeerde beweging, van de keerzijde van het interactiemodel, betekent gewoon dat kerkelijke aspiraties en canonieke regels externe gevolgen kunnen hebben, gevolgen die niet tot het eigen religieuze systeem beperkt blijven. Twee voorbeelden ter illustratie.

In zijn -overigens niet altijd even onbetwiste- biografie van Pius XII, *Hitlers Paus*, beschrijft John Cornwell de drijfveren van de politiek zoals Eugenio Pacelli die voerde, eerst als staatssecretaris, daarna als paus Pius XII[6]. Als een belangrijk fundament voor het concordaat dat in 1933 tussen de Heilige Stoel en Duitsland werd gesloten, voert Cornwell interne kerkpolitieke en canonieke elementen aan. Volgens de auteur uit Cambridge wilde kardinaal Pacelli het centralistische kerkelijk wetboek van 1917 in Duitsland opleggen. Met oude lokale privileges diende daarbij komaf te worden gemaakt. Welnu, die doelstellingen konden het best

---

[6] J. CORNWELL, *Hitlers paus: de verborgen geschiedenis van Pius XII*, Leuven, Van Halewyck, 1999, 415 p.

worden bereikt via een concordaat, dat de kerk en het toen bestaande politieke regime in Duitsland elk op hun terrein het door hen gewenste overwicht verzekerde. Zowel de juridische techniek van het concordaat als de inhoudelijke bevoegdheidsafbakening kwamen beide protagonisten kennelijk goed uit.

Of de analyse van John Cornwell waterdicht is, laat ik in het midden. Opdat ze met zekerheid overeind zou blijven, vergt zij op zijn minst dieper gravend onderzoek. Maar de onderliggende gedachte, of ze nu met de werkelijkheid overeenstemt of niet, is erg interessant. Opties die zich op het terrein van het kerkelijke publiekrecht situeren, zoals de canonieke positie van de paus of van de bisschop, hebben repercussies buiten het canonieke recht. Ze bepalen namelijk de voorkeur voor het concordaat als juridische techniek. Ze sturen bovendien de inhoud van datzelfde concordaat. À la limite wordt het concordaat zowel formeel als inhoudelijk onbegrijpelijk, indien niet eerst een grondige analyse wordt gemaakt van de basisopties die aan het vigerende canoniek recht ten grondslag liggen.

Kritische onderzoekers zouden zelfs de inhoud van een concordaat kunnen aangrijpen om op zoek te gaan naar de *werkelijke* theologische opties van de kerk als instituut. Die vallen immers niet noodzakelijk samen met de officiële retoriek. Eenzelfde analyse kan overigens ook vanuit de invalshoek van de staat worden gemaakt met betrekking tot het inhoudelijke programma waar deze laatste voor staat.

Maar er is niet alleen Pius XII. Er bestaan ook recente dossiers die illustreren hoe het canoniek recht invloed kan uitoefenen op zowel kerk-staat-verhoudingen als profane structuren. Een boeiend voorbeeld, dat trouwens de cirkel rondmaakt, is weerom de profaan-juridische verplichting om elke religieuze ceremonie door een burgerlijk huwelijk te laten voorafgaan.

Deze norm lijkt vandaag wat *passé*. Bovendien staat hij op enigszins gespannen voet met het beginsel van de godsdienstvrijheid[7]. Daarbij komt nog dat de regel, ondanks zijn eerbiedwaardige ouderdom, psychologisch erg moeilijk te verkopen is. Hoe bijvoorbeeld kan aan simpele zielen worden uitgelegd dat ongehuwd samenwonen geen enkel

---

[7] Cf. S. FERRARI, "Church and State in Europe. Common Patterns and Challenges", *European Journal for Church and State Research – Revue européenne des relations Églises-État* 1995, 152; S. FERRARI, "Church and State in Europe. Common Patterns and Challenges", in H.-J. KIDERLEN, H. TEMPEL en R. TORFS (ed.), *Which Relationships Between Churches and the European Union? Thoughts for the Future. Quelles relations entre les Églises et l'Union européenne? Jalons pour l'avenir*, Leuven, Peeters, 1995, 36.

probleem met zich meebrengt en zelfs op profaan-juridische onder-
steuning kan rekenen, terwijl het louter religieuze huwelijk in een aantal
landen nog steeds door de strafwet wordt beteugeld[8]?

Toen in 2001 in België schuchter voorstellen werden gelanceerd om
de verplichte anterioriteit van het burgerlijk huwelijk af te schaffen[9],
bleek ook het Belgische episcopaat niet enthousiast. Waarom? De reac-
tie werd wellicht ingegeven door redenen van canonieke aard, maar dan
canoniek op een tweede niveau. Zoals er een tweede naïviteit bestaat, is
er ook sprake van een canoniek recht op het tweede plan.

Wat betekent dit precies? Wat houdt dat tweede niveau in?

Op het *eerste gezicht* is, althans in dit dossier, elk bisschoppelijk protest onbegrijpelijk. Indien ten minste één van beide partijen katholiek is,
is immers alleen het kerkelijk huwelijk rechtsgeldig. Dat zegt het kerkelijk wetboek[10]. Welke zin heeft het dan op te komen voor een profaanrechtelijk huwelijk dat volgens het eigen systeem niet geldig is en dus
slechts toegang verschaft tot het concubinaat? Eerlijk gezegd, bij een
eerste aanblik geen enkele.

Er is evenwel een *tweede niveau* dat het bisschoppelijke protest
begrijpelijker maakt. Het kerkelijk huwelijk, zoals geregeld door de
canones 1055 tot 1165 van de CIC 1983, besteedt maar weinig zorg aan
de materiële omkadering van het huwelijk[11]. Zorgplicht, levensonder-
houd worden duidelijker en gedetailleerder geregeld door het profane

---

[8] Bijvoorbeeld in België, waar de bedienaar van de eredienst die zich schuldig maakt
aan dit misdrijf volgens artikel 267 van het Strafwetboek kan worden gestraft met een
geldboete en, in geval van recidive, met een gevangenisstraf.

[9] Voorstel van verklaring tot herziening van artikel 21 van de Grondwet, *Parl. St.*
Kamer 2000-2001, nr. 1115/001.

[10] Canon 1059 CIC 1983: "Het huwelijk van katholieken, ook al is maar één partij
katholiek, valt niet alleen onder het goddelijk, maar ook onder het canoniek recht, behoudens de bevoegdheid van de burgerlijke overheid inzake de louter burgerlijke gevolgen
van dit huwelijk."

Canon 1117 CIC 1983: "De boven vastgestelde norm moet in acht genomen worden,
indien ten minste één van beide partijen die het huwelijk sluiten in de katholieke Kerk
gedoopt is of hierin opgenomen en haar niet bij formele akt verlaten heeft, behoudens de
voorschriften van can. 1127, § 2."

[11] Canon 1134 CIC 1983: "Uit een geldig huwelijk ontstaat tussen de echtgenoten een
band, die van nature blijvend en exclusief is; bovendien worden in een christelijk huwelijk de echtgenoten door een bijzonder sacrament voor de plichten en de waardigheid van
hun staat gesterkt en als het ware gewijd."

Canon 1135 CIC 1983: "Ieder van beide echtgenoten heeft gelijke plichten en rechten
met betrekking tot datgene wat tot de gemeenschap van echtelijk leven behoort."

Canon 1136 CIC 1983: "De ouders hebben de zeer ernstige plicht en als eersten het
recht om, zo goed ze kunnen, zowel voor de fysieke, sociale en culturele als voor de
morele en godsdienstige opvoeding van hun kinderen te zorgen."

huwelijksrecht. Dat is natuurlijk wel een interessante gedachte: de zorg-plicht die vanuit een katholiek-ethische hoek met het huwelijk samen-gaat, wordt juridisch krachtdadiger beschermd door het profane huwelijk dan door het katholieke. Het profaanrechtelijke huwelijk dat naar cano-nieke maatstaven *formeel* niet geldig is, heeft *inhoudelijke* troeven die, in de ogen van sommige kerkleiders, de volle steun van de katholieke kerk verdienen.

Nog anders gezegd: de zorgplicht als ethische plicht doet de katho-lieke kerkleiders ten aanzien van het burgerlijk huwelijk een positief standpunt innemen, dat louter formeel-canoniek onbegrijpelijk is, en zelfs schadelijk voor de autonomie van de kerk. Wat geen zin heeft op een eerste niveau, dat van het formele canonieke recht, blijkt opeens uiterst waardevol op een tweede niveau, dat van de inhoudelijke uit-tekening van het huwelijk.

Conclusie: de inhoud van het canoniek recht leidt tot concrete stellingname in het maatschappelijke debat.

TERUGBLIK EN TOEKOMSTPERSPECTIEVEN

Bovenstaand verhaal vertrok van een vaststelling: de lezingen in het raam van de *Monseigneur W. Onclin Chair* handelen geregeld over de verhoudingen tussen kerk en staat. Ook dit jaar is dit het geval voor één van de twee referaten. Het gaat daarbij om een bewuste keuze vanwege de organisatoren. Niet omdat het canoniek recht inhoudelijk arm zou zijn en dringend inspiratie vanuit een profaanrechtelijke hoek zou behoeven. Helemaal niet. Het canoniek recht als succesvol *vehiculum caritatis* baart weinig zorgen. Onder meer kardinaal Sodano is daar duidelijk over.

Dwarsverbindingen met het profane recht hebben echter, ongeacht het geruststellende gezondheidsbulletin van het kerkelijk recht, de laatste tijd iets *onvermijdelijks*, wat hoe dan ook inhoudelijke consequenties voor het canoniek recht zal hebben. Drie fenomenen passeerden in dat raam de revue:

(a) De *traditionele* verhoudingen tussen kerk en staat, typisch voor de negentiende eeuw, waarbij vooral de *afbakening* van bevoegdheden en het trekken van duidelijke demarcatielijnen centraal stond. Type-voorbeeld was de strijd aangaande de jurisdictie over het huwelijk.

(b) De *moderne* verhoudingen tussen kerk en staat waarbij talloze rechtsverhoudingen hun beslag krijgen op het *snijpunt* tussen kerk en staat. Hierbij ontstaat *interactie* tussen twee erg verschillende rechts-systemen waarbij de staat terreinen bezet die hij vroeger braak liet liggen, met in die tijd alle kansen voor de kerk die met een dergelijke houding verbonden waren. Men denke bijvoorbeeld aan binnen-kerkelijke arbeidsverhoudingen.

(c) Het *spiegelbeeld* van de onder (b) beschreven interactie, waarbij, niet slechts juridisch-technisch maar meer nog politiek, binnenker-kelijke opties gevolgen creëren op het terrein van de verhoudingen tussen kerk en staat en van het profane recht. Dat geldt voor de con-cordatenpolitiek van kardinaal Pacelli en voor de houding die kerk-leiders vandaag tegenover het profane huwelijk aannemen.

Anders dan in punt (a), wordt zowel in punt (b) als in punt (c) een systeem beschreven waarin allerlei dwarsverbindingen tussen kerk en staat aan de oppervlakte treden. Het canoniek recht als *vehiculum cari-tatis* ondergaat daar onvermijdelijk een zekere invloed van.

Een verdere vraag is of de hier geschetste evolutie ook haar weerslag vindt of dient te vinden op het vlak van de studie van het kerkelijk recht. Moet daarin meer ruimte geschapen worden voor de studie van kerk-staat verhoudingen? En, indien het antwoord op deze vraag positief is, wat zijn daarvan dan de consequenties voor de nu bestaande opleidin-gen? Dreigen ze minder *internationaal* te worden, wanneer de interactie met ruimtelijk begrensde profane rechtssystemen in toenemende mate aan de orde wordt gesteld?

Die vragen, die een uiterst genuanceerd antwoord verdienen, beant-woord ik verder niet. Ik beperk mij hier tot de wat paradoxale conclusie dat het canoniek recht als *vehiculum caritatis* mogelijk geen intrinsieke nood heeft aan profaanrechtelijke impulsen, maar dat deze laatste nu eenmaal onvermijdelijk op de voorgrond treden in een tijd waarin inter-actie en dwarsverbindingen de juridische verhoudingen tussen kerk en staat ten diepste kleuren.

Een praktische consequentie van dit alles is dat ook in de toekomst kerk-staat-verhoudingen in het raam van de *Monseigneur W. Onclin Chair* aan de orde zullen worden gesteld, uiteraard naast en na het tradi-tionele canoniek recht, dat de hoofdmoot blijft.

CROSS-CONNECTIONS

Rik Torfs

The Monsignor W. Onclin Chair for Comparative Church Law has been in existence since 1990. In the early days, the chair was filled in diverse ways. The most striking was probably a symposium organised by Drs. H. Warnink in the Antwerp Theological and Pastoral Centre (TPC) from 2 to 4 April 1992. That very year, two guest speakers were invited: Brian Ferme who was then still active in Oxford and Frank Lyall from Aberdeen. The following years, reading assignments or other forms of mental gymnastics were devised for students.

The Monsignor W. Onclin Chair, as it now exists, took shape in 1995. The previous improvised approach which had until then been character-istic, with the exception of the aforementioned symposium in the TPC, was abandoned. From then on, two internationally renowned academics were invited every year, each of whom gave a week of lectures. At the end of this week, during an academic session, they expressed their ideas on a topic currently the focus of their academic interest. These lectures were also published.

Apart from the undisputed competence, the two speakers did not necessarily have a great deal in common. This has been clear from the very start. Take 1995 for instance, with Mgr. Cormac Burke, Rota Audi-tor, specialist in marriage law, and Professor Ruud Huysmans, rather an expert in church structures and fully au fait with the ins and outs of the institution in our modern society. Burke-Huysmans thus became the first surprising pair produced by the Monsignor W. Onclin Chair – and it would not be the last. Subsequent combinations, together with the titles of their lectures, can be found on the closing pages of this booklet: Ser-rano-Morrisey, Pree-Provost, Örsy-Coertzen, Migliore-Wood, Beal-Papasthatis, Coriden-Pagé. Great names without a doubt but also, such diversity.

This colourfulness is also reflected in the problems finding titles for the annual publications. If only we had chosen simple numbering right from the word go, such as Monsignor W. Onclin Chair 1, then 2, 3 and 4, etc., in the same way that constructivist paintings often are just given a number. Construction 4 – no pathos, no fuss. But no, we chose to use a great title, right from the start, with all the associated consequences: for example, *In Diversitate Unitas* (1997) or *Bridging Past and Future* (1998). Such titles show that the publications attached to the Monsignor W. Onclin chair are not rigidly structured subject editions, but a fairly loose collection of texts.

Some obligatory post-modern comments on this lack of unity can always be formulated to please the fanatics of the genre, for instance: the booklets published within the context of the Monsignor W. Onclin Chair give a warning in their structure – or lack of it – of a false harmony model. They show that *unity*, even in canon law, is no longer to be taken for granted, and may well be an exercise for anyone who regards it as desirable as an end result.

This lack of internal unity could roughly be reported in this way – somewhat academically and no less pedantically. However, this kind of explanation would imply a distortion of reality. Post-modern objectives have never been pursued by the Monsignor W. Onclin Chair organisation. Going along with trends in this direction, including accents on the fragmentary and the situated subject – sometimes, a little toned down, *pour les besoins de la cause* – has not been practised at any time. Incidentally, canon law as an academic discipline is perhaps not so fragmented. In this respect, in the context of the Onclin Chair, we have no opinion whatsoever.

What we do all at least implicitly believe in – as the recent history of the Monsignor W. Onclin Chair reveals – is a diversity of approaches and an abundance of study material, which are important for dealing creatively with canon law. In particular, since 1995, the contribution of church/state specialists has been explicitly visible. Among the authors who have had a paper published since then, some are first and foremost experts in the legal relationships between church and state, such as Ch. Papasthatis and J.E. Wood, while others straddle the fields of canon law and church/state relations. The article by J. Tretera also emphasises what is known in Germany as *Staatskirchenrecht*.

In brief, the varied texts which represent the fruits of seven Onclin Chairs have nothing to do with any (watered-down) post-modern vision of how canon law functions or should function. The academic or theological status of canon law remains outside the equation.

The diversity and multiplicity of texts refer to something quite different. Canon law – regardless of its exact nature – does not operate in a vacuum, it is not an exotic plant, it is not a lofty matter entirely beyond the grasp of any outsider. On the contrary, as a science and as a practical discipline, canon law is given form through a dialogue with the surrounding environment. The legal relationships between church and state play a major role, even an indispensable role, in this respect.

Once again, therefore, the wide spectrum which covers the texts published within the context of the Monsignor W. Onclin Chair is *not* a consequence of a well-defined (fragmentary) conception of canon law, seen internally. No, the multiplicity refers to the necessary openness which canon law has to display to the outside world, first and foremost to the legal relations between church and state.

It is difficult to deny that, in the long term, this openness can have consequences for the identity of canon law. In the same way that a person who travels or reads begins to think differently about certain things, usually without noticing, an open canon law is influenced in the long term by the disciplines or impulses to which it lays itself open. The internal state of health of canon law is not really a decisive factor in this process.

Again, a canon law which is methodologically *drifting* may well draw lessons from developments in civil law, trends in sociology, or movements in the legal relationships between church and state. But this is no less true for a *flourishing* canon law, which is in no way in crisis and which is apparently satisfied with itself. This type of canon law is also influenced by all kinds of cross connections, particularly those arising in the sphere of the relations between church and state.

At this point in history, we apparently find ourselves in the second hypothesis. Canon law is not gasping for breath but is, according to all the official sources, undergoing a period of vitality. In November 2001, the tenth anniversary of the CCEO was marked by a large-scale symposium held in Rome. At this gathering, the law of the church was awarded the distinction *vehiculum caritatis*. During a speech delivered on 22 November 2001, Cardinal Angelo Sodano recounted how happy Pope John-Paul II was with this designation. It may be clear that a legal system to which the description *vehiculum caritatis* can be applied can take solace in its excellent state of health. Many secular legal systems have to make do with less.

Nevertheless, despite this optimistic point of departure, many kinds of cross connections are clearly evident between canon law on the one hand and the legal relationships between church and state on the other hand.

CHURCH AND STATE ON TWO FRONTS

The inevitable character of church/state relationships – incidentally, just like the urgency with which they emerge and where cross connections arise with canon law – has not always been as self-evident in the past.

Until well into the twentieth century, the legal relationships between church and state in Europe were characterised by a strong tendency towards *demarcation*. The rules determined especially who was competent in which matter. A typical example is legal competence with respect to marriage. In various European countries, the law or constitution contained the principle that a civil marriage was necessary before any religious ceremony could take place[1]. Such a provision exposes the balance of power and assigns competence, but does not take into consideration any approach to the *content* of the marriage. In other respects, the nineteenth century saw less discussion on this topic than today. Marriage was a respectable institution, whether it was legally in the hands of the church or controlled by the state. Virtually no room was left for the *à la carte* requirements of those eager to marry. Only later did civil marriage move away from religious marriage: the latter remained in principle indissoluble. In brief, the legal relationships between church and state, the demarcation of powers relating to marriage, did not immediately lead to cross connections between the content of canon law and certain secular legal trends.

This observation is not so strange. Church and state relationships once exerted an influence at a high level, the level of power and authority. The debates were played out in an atmosphere of competition. Cooperation in terms of the content of specific cases remained rare.

This cooperation is now in full swing and church and state appear to be partners and not just rivals – partners who are both regularly involved with the same cases, institutes and social phenomena.

A clear example of this evolution are labour relations within the church, such as the status of a lay person working professionally in the pastoral domain[2]. This person's legal position usually includes both

---

[1] In Belgium, the principle can be found in Article 21 of the Constitution, in the Netherlands in Article 1:68 of the Civil Code, in France and Germany in ordinary legislation.

[2] A. BORRAS (ed.), *Des laïcs en responsabilité pastorale? Accueillir de nouveaux ministères*, Paris, Cerf, 1998, 313 pp.; R. TORFS and K. MARTENS (eds.), *Parochieassistenten. Leken als bedienaar van de eredienst?*, in R. TORFS (ed.), *Scripta canonica*, I, Leuven, Peeters, 1998, x + 142 pp.; R. TORFS, "Les assistants paroissiaux rémunérés par l'État en Belgique", *Quaderni di diritto e politica ecclesiastica* 1998, 255-268.

canon law and secular law aspects, where the balance between the two aspects is both important and delicate[3]. The canonical status must take account of the basic principles of secular labour law. The labour contract, in turn, should provide room for the religious dimension of the working relationship. Again, the status of the pastoral worker is something of a patchwork in which secular law aspects are important, as well as canonical elements. The legal relationships between church and state determine whether and to what extent the internal church relationships are influenced or coloured by the protection mechanisms of secular labour law.

This question can produce particularly subtle answers. Canon law and secular law are not each assigned their own place, as was the case in the battle for competence relating to marriage. The motto is no longer the rather narrow-minded *chaque chose à sa place, et une place pour chaque chose*. On the contrary, room is created for mixed domains in which church and state can meet and both legal systems are linked together in some way.

This type of precision work occurs regularly in modern church/state relationships. This involves two systems, each with a distinct internal dynamism, i.e. the more pragmatic secular law and its canonical counterpart, neither more nor less of a *vehiculum caritatis*. The labour law referred to above provides a fine example of this interaction.

Liability law provides another good illustration. In countries which have the tradition of a civil code, the principal is liable for damage caused under certain circumstances by his subordinate. The principal/subordinate relationship is broader than the pure labour contract, that much is certain. But does it also encompass the relationship between a *bishop* and a *pastor*? In other words, does the canonical *bishop/pastor* relationship fit into the secular *principal/subordinate* picture[4]? It is unnecessary to add that such an issue requires a detailed analysis of both

---

[3] Not in all countries – Germany has more autonomy.

[4] Cf. the relevant jurisdiction: Brussels Correctional Court, 9 April 1998, *Journal des tribunaux* 1998, 530, amended by Court of Appeal Brussels 25 September 1998. *Journal des tribunaux* 1998, 712; Dendermonde Correctional Court, 10 June 1998, *Revue générale de droit civil belge* 1998, 339. Some legal doctrine thinks, based on these few decisions, that it can talk of an established jurisdiction which rejects this link: see in this respect L.-L. CHRISTIANS, "L'autorité religieuse entre stéréotype napoléonien et exégèse canonique : l'absence de responsabilité objective de l'évêque pour son clergé en droit belge", *Quaderni di diritto e politica ecclesiastica* 2000, 951-960. This conclusion seems to us somewhat premature, all the more since the Supreme Court (*Cour de Cassation*) has not yet made a decision on this important legal question.

relationships, ultimately including a comparison. Given the nature of the two legal systems, this comparison will always fall somewhat short, but nonetheless needs a clear answer, i.e. yes or no. *Yes* implies that the bishop can possibly be held liable for certain forms of harm caused to others by the pastor. *No* means the reverse.

It may be clear that in both the examples quoted, i.e. the status of the pastoral worker and the liability case, the cross connections between the canonical and secular systems are both subtle and delicate. The somewhat distant demarcation of competence which is so typical of the nineteenth century has now given way to a refined form of interaction as a result of all kinds of specific cases.

Increasing *interaction* is therefore an important characteristic of today's church/state relationships. Secular desiderata and techniques are thus slowly penetrating into canon law, even if the latter is a *vehiculum caritatis* which makes it excellent, from a purely intrinsic point of view, and which does not feel the need for all kinds of external input. Since this is also clear: the state and secular law are the inquiring party. In an increasingly regulated society, the civil authorities find that some mechanisms which provide citizens with protection cannot remain entirely absent in a religious context either[5]. In other words, rather than the nineteenth-century *demarcation*, we now have *interaction*, but it is interaction where the state makes a move, is clearly taking the initiative, is promulgating imperative standards in fields which, from a legal point of view, used to be *fallow land*. This fallow land which allowed religious communities to stick rigidly to their own course, based on their religious beliefs.

CHURCH AND STATE ON THREE FRONTS

However, the church is not always on the defensive. Admittedly, this may be how it seems when the two phases outlined above are taken into consideration: a fairly balanced *demarcation period* (cf. the battle for jurisdiction regarding marriage) is followed by an *interaction period* during which the state imposes requirements in fields which used legally to be fallow land. The church is apparently readjusting.

---

[5] R. TORFS, "The Roman Catholic Church and Secular Legal Culture in the Twentieth Century", *Studia Historiae Ecclesiasticae* 1999, 1-20.

Apparently: in the same way that the state's aspirations can have consequences in an area which used to be the exclusive domain of the church, the reverse movement is also conceivable, i.e. a movement in which the church, based on its self-understanding, weighs in on the legal relationships between church and state and, ultimately, even on secular law.

The fact that the reverse movement therefore also seems to exist does not mean, even implicitly, that church and state are at the same level and that the church must therefore be regarded as a *societas perfecta*. The existence of the reverse movement, from the flip-side of the interaction model, simply means that ecclesiastical aspirations and canonical rules can have external consequences, consequences which do not remain confined to that religious system. We quote two examples to illustrate this point.

John Cornwell, in his biography of Pius XII, *Hitler's Pope* (which is not incidentally as undisputed in all respects), describes the driving forces of the policy pursued by Eugenio Pacelli, first as secretary of state, then as Pope Pius XII[6]. Cornwell quotes internal church politics and canonical elements as an important foundation of the concordat concluded between the Vatican and Germany in 1933. According to the Cambridge author, Cardinal Pacelli wanted to impose the centralist code of canon law of 1917 in Germany. An end would have to be put to old local privileges. Well, these objectives could best be achieved by a concordat which guaranteed both the church and the political regime of the day in Germany the authority each desired in its own domain. Evidently, both protagonists benefited from both the legal technique of the concordat and its intrinsic demarcation of authority.

I leave open the question of whether John Cornwell's analysis is watertight. Further-reaching research, at least, is needed for it to stand its ground. However, the underlying idea – whether or not it corresponds to reality – is very interesting. Options in the field of public law of the church, such as the canonical position of the Pope or the bishop, have repercussions outside canon law. Specifically, they define the preference for the concordat as a legal technique. Moreover, they steer the contents of that same concordat. Ultimately, the concordat becomes incomprehensible both formally and in terms of content if a thorough analysis is not first performed of the basic options underlying the canon law currently in force.

---

[6] J. CORNWELL, *Hitler's Pope: the Secret History of Pius XII*, New York, Viking, 1999, xii + 430 pp.

Critical researchers could even take hold of the content of a concordat in order to look for the *actual* theological options of the church as an institution. After all, these do not always coincide with the official rhetoric. The same analysis can of course also be made from the angle of the state with respect to the programme of content it advocates.

However, the care of Pius XII is not the only one. Recent cases also exist which illustrate how canon law can exert an influence both on church/state relationships and secular structures. One prime example and one which completes the circle is again the secular law obligation that every religious marriage ceremony be preceded by a civil marriage.

Today, this norm seems somewhat *passé*. Moreover, it is to some extent at odds with the principle of religious freedom[7]. In addition, the ruling is psychologically very difficult to sell, despite its venerable old age. How, for example, can it be explained to simple people that living together outside marriage poses no problem whatsoever and can even rely on support from secular law, while purely religious marriage is still curbed by criminal law in some countries[8]?

When tentative proposals were made in Belgium in 2001 to abolish compulsory prior civil marriage[9], even the Belgian episcopacy was less than enthusiastic. Why? The reaction was probably based on reasons of a canonical nature, but canonical at a second level. In the same way as a second naivety exists, canon law on a second level also exists.

What exactly does this mean? What does this second level imply?

At *first sight*, at least in this case, any episcopal protest is incomprehensible. After all, if at least one of the two parties is Catholic, only a church marriage is lawfully valid between baptised persons. This is written in canon law[10]. What is then the sense of taking the defence of a

---

[7] Cf. S. FERRARI, "Church and State in Europe. Common Patterns and Challenges", *European Journal for Church and State Research – Revue européenne des relations Églises-État* 1995, 152; S. FERRARI, "Church and State in Europe. Common Patterns and Challenges", in H.-J. KIDERLEN, H. TEMPEL and R. TORFS (ed.), *Which Relationships Between Churches and the European Union? Thoughts for the Future. Quelles relations entre les Églises et l'Union européenne? Jalons pour l'avenir*, Leuven, Peeters, 1995, 36.

[8] For example, in Belgium, where the minister of worship who commits this crime under Article 267 of the Criminal Code can be punished by a fine and, if he repeats the offence, can be imprisoned.

[9] Proposed declaration to review Article 21 of the Constitution, *Parl. St.* Kamer 2000-2001, no. 1115/001.

[10] Canon 1059 CIC 1983: "Even if only one party is Catholic, the marriage of Catholics is governed not only by divine law but also by canon law, without prejudice to the competence of civil authority concerning the merely civil effects of the same marriage."

secular law marriage which is invalid in their own canonical system and therefore only grants access to concubinage? Honestly speaking, at first sight, no sense at all.

However, the episcopal objection becomes more understandable at a *second level*. A church marriage, as governed by canons 1055 to 1165 of the CIC 1983, devotes only scant attention to the material context of the marriage[11]. The duty of care and support are more clearly and meticulously governed by secular marriage law. This is of course an interesting thought: the duty of care associated with marriage from the Catholic/ethical angle is more forcefully protected from a legal point of view by a secular marriage than by a Catholic marriage. A secular law marriage which is not *formally* valid by canonical criteria has assets in terms of *content* which, in the eyes of some church leaders, deserve the full backing of the Catholic church.

To put it yet another way: the duty of care as an ethical duty causes the Catholic church leaders to adopt a positive attitude towards civil marriage, which is from a purely formal canonical angle incomprehensible and even harmful for the autonomy of the church. What may make no sense at the first level – that of formal canon law – suddenly seems extremely valuable at a second level – detailing the content of the marriage.

Conclusion: the content of canon law leads to specific attitudes in the social debate.

LOOKING BACK AND LOOKING AHEAD

The above account began with an observation, that the lectures given within the context of the Monsignor W. Onclin Chair regularly touch on

---

Canon 1117 CIC 1983: "The form established above must be observed if at least one of the parties contracting marriage was baptized in the Catholic Church or received into it and has not defected from it by a formal act, without prejudice to the prescripts of can. 1127, § 2."

[11] Canon 1134 CIC 1983: "From a valid marriage there arises between the spouses a bond which by its nature is perpetual and exclusive. Moreover, a special sacrament strengthens and, as it were, consecrates the spouses in a Christian marriage for the duties and dignity of their state."

Canon 1135 CIC 1983: "Each spouse has an equal duty and right to those things which belong to the partnership of conjugal life."

Canon 1136 CIC 1983: "Parents have the most grave duty and the primary right to take care as best they can for the physical, social, cultural, moral, and religious education of their offspring."

the relationships between church and state. This year, this is also true of one of the two papers. This is a conscious choice by the organisers; not because canon law is poor in terms of content and urgently needs inspiration from a secular law angle. Not at all. Canon law as a successful *vehiculum caritatis* gives little cause for concern. Cardinal Sodano, for one, is clear on this matter.

Recently, however, cross connections with secular law, despite the reassuring health report on canon law, have had a sense of *inevitability*, which will in some way have consequences in terms of content for canon law. In this context, three phenomena were reviewed:

(a) the *traditional* relationships between church and state, typical of the nineteenth century, focusing in particular on the demarcation of powers and drawing clear demarcation lines. A typical example was the struggle for jurisdiction over marriage;

(b) the *modern* relationships between church and state, in which numerous legal relationships have an effect at the *intersection* between church and state. This creates interaction between two very different legal systems, where the state occupies territory which it previously left lying fallow, with all the opportunities for the church associated with such an attitude at that time. We can think for example of internal church labour relations;

(c) the *mirror image* of the interaction described under (b), where internal church options create consequences – from a legal as well as a political point of view – in the area of the relationships between church and state and of secular law. This applies to the concordat policy of Cardinal Pacelli and to the attitude adopted by church leaders today to secular marriage.

Unlike point (a), both points (b) and (c) describe a system in which all kinds of cross connections between church and state rise to the surface. Canon law as a *vehiculum caritatis* inevitably feels the influence of this to some extent.

One further question is whether the development outlined here also has or should have repercussions at the level of the study of canon law. Should more room be created here for the study of church/state relationships? Should the answer to this question be positive, what are the consequences of this for existing canon law programmes? Do they risk becoming less *international* if the interaction with spatially limited secular legal systems is increasingly a subject for discussion?

These questions which deserve an extremely subtle answer, will not be answered further here. I confine myself at this stage to the somewhat paradoxical conclusion that canon law as a *vehiculum caritatis* perhaps has no intrinsic need for secular law impulses, but that the latter move inevitably to the forefront at a time when interaction and cross connections are most deeply influencing the legal relationships between church and state.

One practical consequence of all this is that church/state relationships will continue to be discussed in the future within the context of the Monsignor W. Onclin Chair, alongside traditional canon law of course, which remains its principal concern.

SYSTEMS OF RELATIONS BETWEEN THE STATE AND CHURCHES IN GENERAL (SYSTEMS OF STATE ECCLESIASTICAL LAW) AND THEIR OCCURRENCE IN THE CZECH LANDS IN PARTICULAR

JIŘÍ RAJMUND TRETERA

1. SYSTEMS OF RELATIONS BETWEEN THE STATE AND CHURCHES IN GENERAL (STATE ECCLESIASTICAL LAW SYSTEMS)

1.1 The Confessional State

1.1.1 The Classical Confessional State

The term "confessional state" means the relational arrangement between churches and the state in which state authorities favour one religion, or only one denomination within the scope of a certain religion. The state either completely rules out, or merely tolerates the profession of other religions and denominations or the condition of being nondenominational. On the basis of these two alternatives it is possible to distinguish between confessional states without toleration and those with toleration.

Since the beginning of the 19th century confessional state systems without toleration have occurred only rarely. As a rule, toleration in confessional states is significantly limited. It extends to only some denominations and religions and *eo ipso* means inequality between the favoured church or religious society on the one hand and the tolerated churches or religious societies on the other[1]. Degrees of toleration and inequality can be diverse. Therefore, the division of confessional states into those with toleration and those without toleration is a determination of the formal legal character of a state's confessional arrangement, rather than an expression of tolerance in the sense of an attitude toward living that prevails in a country.

---

[1] The favoured church does not always have to be called the "state church," and conversely the formal continuation of a church that is designated as a "state church" does not always mean that this is an instance of a confessional state system.

1.1.2 The Confessional State "à rebours"

States in which some atheistic ideology plays the role of a religion are usually classified as confessional states in the current science of state ecclesiastical law. Because the ideology is favoured in a way similar to that of religion in a confessional state, it is possible to say that the ideology is a religion in a negative sense.

In this way, "the Communist states were essentially confessional states à rebours (in the reverse direction) because they imposed atheistic ideology on the whole society as an official religion"[2]. The enforcement of Marxist-Leninist ideology as a so-called "scientific" worldview, of which atheism is an undeniable constituent part, was still a fact of life a decade ago in the socialist states of central and eastern Europe. The ideology was presented by the actual dictatorship of the Communist party, and was supported by legal measures enacted in these states, and sometimes also by the constitutionally guaranteed "leading role"[3] of the party. A huge portion of humanity still lives under such confessional states à rebours, as in the communist countries of eastern Asia and Cuba.

If we consider the outward manifestations of the governing atheistic ideology in the above-mentioned states, we frequently notice that they did not lack definite cultic elements. Some of the ordinary civic ceremonies in these states were turned into overblown rituals that replaced classical displays of religious worship, with the goal of completely displacing them. For example, May Day parades in which pictures or paper statues of the classic figures of Marxism-Leninism were on display were strongly reminiscent of religious processions with icons. The civic ceremonies of welcoming infant citizens and marriage copied similar church ceremonies.

Communists adapted the details of traditional customary ceremonies from the main religious denomination in each country that they controlled. In the former GDR – a predominantly Protestant country – confirmation was a very important religious event in the coming of age of young Lutherans. It was displaced by a civic "initiation of youth" (Jugendweihe). In the former Czechoslovakia, Catholic confirmation

---

[2] Józef KRUKOWSKI, "Aktuální otázky polského konfesního práva" [Current Questions in Polish State Ecclesiastical Law], Revue církevního práva – Church Law Review, 11 (3/1998), 150.

[3] In Czechoslovakia, the dictatorship held this power from February 25, 1948, and the "leading role" of the party exerted influence from July 11, 1960 to November 28, 1989.

was replaced by a similar, somewhat less solemn, civil ceremony of the distribution of citizenship identity cards to teenagers.

At public meetings and rallies, Communist speakers "preached" their "sermons," and everyone joined in the common singing of political songs. In practice, attendance at these events was compulsory, especially for employees, students, apprentices, and pupils. Some of these songs, such as "The Song of Work," had the melody and verbal cadence of a religious hymn. The imparting of atheistic science became an aspect of ordinary teaching, especially for those subjects that had this topic in their lesson plans. For this reason, too, many believing teachers lost their jobs, and believers were not permitted to undertake pedagogical studies, since teachers had the mission of being, among other things, "priests of atheism."

Of course, some religious freedoms were permitted in Communist countries, especially concerning the performing of simple ceremonies. This was quite certainly the case after public displays of religious attitudes and faith had been "driven into church buildings and sacristies."

The degree of this "tolerance" varied in different Communist countries, which again recalls the above-mentioned older pattern of the confessional state. But in this case, it was more a matter of a distinctively temporary "tolerance." The theory of "scientific" Communism never hid the fact that a certain tolerance of "filling the religious needs"[4] of a "backward" segment of the population was only a temporary tactic in the long-term strategy of the Communist movement. The final aim of the movement always remained a total liquidation of churches and religion. In the autumn of 1968, the Albanian Socialist Republic reached the point of a constitutional ban on displays of religious activity of any kind and the legal suppression of all denominations and religious societies. As a result, all churches and mosques in the nation were closed. Albanian Communists were ahead of other Communist parties in the establishment of a confessional state à rebours without toleration.

In history it is possible to find other and older examples of confessional states à rebours. One example is the atheistic dictatorship of Mexico in the first half of the 20th century. There are also other states with a single governing ideology that did not include atheism as one of

---

[4] The phrase "filling religious needs" was intended to be (and is) offensive to believers. Therefore, we do not recommend its use. Faith is not an item of consumer goods, while mere participation in religious services is not enough to fulfil the personality of a believer.

its constituent parts, but which bore certain quasi-religious features. As examples we can mention the reign of the "Cult of Reason" during the Jacobin dictatorship of the French Revolution (1793-94) or the "Cult of Blood and Soil" during the Nazi regime in Germany (1933-45).

1.2 The Secular State

1.2.1 Confessional Neutrality, but not Values Neutrality, of the Secular State

What has prevailed in modern states is the idea of religious freedom, and with it the postulation of confessional neutrality, but not values neutrality, of the state. There has been a transition from a state being directed to the support of a certain confession, thereby identifying with that confession, to a state with confessional neutrality, that is, with worldly or secular neutrality. The assumption here is that this kind of state does not identify with any denomination, religious faith, or atheistic ideology.

Another important characteristic of the secular state is a system of equal treatment or parity. The state deals with all recognized religions and confessions on an equal basis. All religions and confessions have the right to be recognized and treated in the same way if they meet the conditions laid down in the law.

Sometimes we meet cases of a secular state in which the system of parity is not applied consistently. Such, for example, are two countries of the British Isles. The Church of England is identified as the established church in England, and the Presbyterian Church has a similar position in Scotland. In actual fact, religious freedom in both England and Scotland is so great and so extensive that these countries are almost indistinguishable from secular states that apply the parity system consistently.

The last country in Europe with a church designated explicitly as the "state church" was Sweden. That changed on January 1, 2000, when the law releasing the Swedish Lutheran Church from the position of state church went into effect.

The confessional neutrality of a modern secular state does not mean, however, that it is neutral regarding values. It is in the interest of all citizens that the state recognizes the positive contribution of religious societies and does not interfere with their activities. It is even further in the citizens' interest that the state supports and possibly collaborates with some activities of religious societies, provided that such support and collaboration is appropriate and in keeping with the principle of parity.

According to the degree of support and collaboration, the theory of state ecclesiastical law divides secular states into two categories: secular states with separation of church and state, and secular states with cooperation between church and state. As we will show below, what is involved here is a division of a historical character. Today, these two groups of secular states are steadily moving closer to resembling one another, even while significant internal differences remain within each of them.

1.2.2 The Secular State with Separation of Church and State

In the past there was a great deal of discussion of the need for separation of church and state, and even of the dissociation of church and state. Separation was supposed to

1) Remove unpleasant (and unnecessary) interference of the state in church affairs. This would give all religious societies equal status, both among themselves and with regard to other organizations of a non-religious character.

2) By this means, however, an effort to drive churches to the margins of society had been advanced in some countries. This effort was motivated by anti-church passions and anti-religious intolerance.

Today, the term "separation of church and state" is used for the system of state ecclesiastical law in the USA, based on the First Amendment to the Constitution (1791); in Brazil, according to the decree of 1890; in France, according to the 1905 Law of Separation; and in two out of the 26 Swiss cantons[5]. In the cases of Brazil and the USA, a friendly type of church-state separation was under discussion, whereas the French model of separation was considered hostile to churches. Portugal also took on the character of a secular state with separation of church and state (as well as having a spirit unfriendly to the church) for a period (1911-35).

Some historians characterize the disestablishment in Ireland (1871) and Wales (1921) as separation. In fact, these countries became secular states with church-state cooperation where the principle of parity is observed consistently. These states replaced confessional states in which the Anglican Church had been "established" in both countries.

The term *Trennung* is also used in the legal provisions of the Federal Republic of Germany. German legal theorists use the term "coordina-

---

[5] The Canton of Genève (from 1907), and the Canton of Neuchâtel (from 1943).

tive" or "cooperative" separation. The state, in which the majority of churches have the standing of "public-service" corporations, collects church tax from church members. However, Germany cannot be ranked as a classic state with church-state separation.

The term "separation" was also used after the Bolshevik coup d'état in Russia. In actuality, the system that was installed was not a secular state with separation of church and state or a religiously and ideologically neutral world-view. It was an ideologically atheistic state, that is, a confessional state *à rebours* in the negative sense. The so-called "separation" was only an external formality. Hidden behind it was a powerful system of control by several state organs that administered religious structures while simultaneously and progressively liquidating them.

Similarly, in several other countries where the Communists later took control (such as the GDR, Poland, and Hungary,) a Soviet-style "separation" was proclaimed. In others (Czechoslovakia, Romania, and Bulgaria), the expression "separation" was not used. In this respect, there did exist certain small differences in state ecclesiastical law among the countries of the Soviet bloc, but on the level of practice the division of these countries into states "with separation" and "without separation" would have had no substantial basis.

On the whole, the concept of church-state separation is not clear and equivocal. A separation never was, nor is at this time, the prevailing model of church-state relations. Perhaps this is why the term does not figure in contemporary documents of international law.

1.2.3 The Secular State with Cooperation between Church and State

In the large majority of democratic states, relations between the state and religious communities must be characterized as systems of non-identification and simultaneous cooperation, especially in matters of common interest (schools, health care, and social welfare).

We meet various forms of church support (for example, in the area of taxes) even in states with separation, as well as with various manifestations of cooperation: appointment of military chaplains, support of church schools, sometimes even recognition of church marriages (for example, in the USA). However, in states with cooperation between church and state, this kind of cooperation is presumed to a much larger extent and legally regulated in greater detail.

The need for social support and cooperation of churches and religious societies is based on the experience that the religious activity proper to these churches and societies is extraordinarily important and useful for their members, who in this way are granted civil freedom in an area most significant to them. Yet, even for those citizens who do not belong to the churches or societies, this activity does not lack meaning, as it is a contribution that benefits them as well.

It is impossible not to see the extent of the services churches and religious societies furnish to society as a whole, such as:

1) assisting in the fight against, and prevention of, crime and drug abuse,
2) rehabilitation provided for released prisoners, the care of the homeless and refugees,
3) the care of the elderly and powerless provided in the Christian spirit of charitable activities,
4) the care of the incurably ill in hospices staffed by dedicated church members,
5) strengthening the stability of marriage and the family,
6) protecting human life and dignity, fostering an attitude of harmony with nature and the environment, or
7) serving as important co-creators of national culture.

Churches and religious societies can also further the work of society by spreading their faith as a prevention of the harmful influence of certain extremist religious groups, or as active promoters of tourism (such as in trips to pilgrimage places, international church gatherings, visits to churches, monasteries, and historic religious sites.) A historic religious site that is living, still functioning, and still serving its original purpose is more attractive and interesting than a building preserved as a museum. The absence of churches and their widespread work in society would be a severe loss for the whole society. For this reason, direct reference is sometimes made to "the irreplaceable role of the churches in society"[6].

Almost all states of the European Union belong to the class of secular states with church-state cooperation. France, the USA, and Brazil are converging to the system of cooperation and in large measure are states "with separation" in name only. At the same time it is possible to note the transformation of a confessional state to a secular state with church-state cooperation in contemporary Greece. The former Communist states are passing from having atheistic state systems to a religiously neutral order with a predominantly cooperative direction.

---

[6] State leaders used this expression in the past. In the years 1999-2001, representatives of the churches in the expert commission of the government ministry proposed that this formulation be used as a part of the preamble of the new law on churches.

1.2.3 The So-called "Lay State"

At times the term "secular state" is used interchangeably with the term "lay state." Conceivably, this happens because of a careless translation of the French *état laïque*, and is lacking in definition. It is necessary to proceed from the meaning of "lay person." In the original meaning, a lay person is someone who is not a cleric or priest. A secular state, however, is not the opposite of a "clerical state" ruled by priests[7], but rather is in opposition to a confessional state, that is, a state whose authorities, whether or not they are priests, favour a certain denomination or ideology. The opposite of a confessional state, therefore, is not a "lay state" but a secular state, which is confessionally neutral and which is not partial to any denomination or absence of a denomination, including an atheistic ideology.

Therefore, we do not recommend using the uncertain and unclear expression "lay state," or at least we recommend avoiding the expression in scientific and legislative work. In view of its emotional charge, it is probably unrealistic to expect that the term will disappear completely from the language of journalists, with their penchant for emotional turns of phrase.

2.   THE STATE AND CHURCHES IN THE CZECH LANDS FROM THE ENLIGHTENMENT TO THE PRESENT

2.1 The Period of Jurisdictionalism and a Confessional State (1620-1848)

The state ecclesiastical system in Bohemia and Moravia under Habsburg rule after 1620 was that of a Catholic confessional state. The Jews were the only tolerated minority. This toleration was limited, and their situation gradually worsened, especially during the first half of the 18th century. Only the territory of Aš (a part of Egerland) was exempt from

---

[7] A confessional state was not a state governed by priests or clerics. Not even the Papal States could be taken as a clerical state in the strict meaning of the term. The Papal States in central Italy were liquidated in 1870 as a result of the Italian occupation. This was in past centuries the only state in which the government was in the hands of church representatives. The characterization of Vatican City, which has existed since 1929, is discussed elsewhere. Specific characterization of the Tibetan state during the period when the Dalai Lama exercised secular power is outside the scope of the present considerations.

the exclusive legitimacy of Catholicism; in this small region, the Lutheran Protestant Church, too, had a free and state-supported position.

In Silesia, the third of the lands of the Czech crown, the Catholic Church had a privileged status after 1620. However, as time passed, Lutheran Protestants enjoyed episodes of varying degrees of toleration.

During this period, the ruling dynasty also began to change its relation to the Catholic Church in the spirit of the doctrine of jurisdictionalism. According to this doctrine, the secular ruler has the so-called *iura maiestatica circa sacra,* that is, the sole right to determine the regulations governing the relation between the state and the church without regard for the actual interests and needs of the church, even while outwardly showing favour to the church. (In Protestant countries, the ruler could moreover usurp the *iura maiestatica in sacra,* the right to intervene in dogmatic matters, and the *ius reformandi,* the right to reform the church.)

The subordination of the church to state power justified by jurisdictionalism was advanced even more emphatically in the 18th century, this time from the position of enlightened absolutism, which understood the church as a part of the machinery of government.

From the start of the 18th century there was a marked limitation of the church in property affairs due to repeated state financial crises.

The jurisdiction of church courts was progressively restricted, starting again with property matters. During the reign of Maria Theresa, these restrictions limited the autonomy of church courts in marriage cases and in criminal cases against clerics, thereby attaining a serious breach of the *privilegia fori.*

It was already the case before 1620 that the ruler had the right to nominate archbishops of Prague. This right was extended to other newly established dioceses, so that the free choice of bishops by a cathedral chapter was preserved only in the diocese of Olomouc (raised to the rank of an archdiocese in 1777).

The Catholic Church in the Czech Lands was also restricted in its relations with foreign institutions. The *placet regium,* the right of state control over publication of church decrees, had already been established before 1620. In the 18th century, correspondence of the clergy with Rome could be conducted only through the agency of the imperial state council.

During the years between 1780 and 1790, Joseph II intensified state control over churches. In his effort to regulate church life down to the tiniest detail, he went so far as to promulgate a decree on liturgical matters. He specified, for example, the Sunday on which the Mass in honour of the dedication of the local church was to be celebrated in places where the day of dedication was not known. He limited the number of church feast days and interfered in other ways with the liturgical calendar. He stipulated how many altar candles were to be lit on a given day. Particularly odious was his ruling that burial in coffins was forbidden (presumably to save wood) and to be replaced by burial in bags. Even persons close to the emperor criticized him for this measure, and he repealed it before he died.

Acts of Toleration

Joseph's legislative acts of toleration can be considered as an improvement of the situation and a step toward more justice in the ordering of religious affairs. The shadow side of the acts was that they provided only a limited toleration. The Catholic Church had a privileged status, even though it was greatly circumscribed by binding state legislation, and its own statutes only had limited force. Some Protestant historians suggest that the so-called "period of toleration" (1781-1861) was merely a continuation of "re-catholicising" under a different guise.

It is certain that the motivation of Joseph II for these interventions was the ideas of the Enlightenment. Another reason that has been advanced is the effort to dissuade secret Protestants (who were usually German) from leaving the country, and conversely to enable immigration from German Protestant lands, thereby strengthening Germanization efforts within the monarchy.

The Act of Toleration of October 13, 1781 allowed the functioning in the Czech Lands of the Protestant churches of the Augsburg Confession and the Helvetian Confession and the Orthodox Church. On the basis of the Act of Toleration, 78,000 inhabitants of Bohemia and Moravia declared their membership in Protestant churches, and gradually 73 Protestant parish communities of either the Augsburg or Helvetian Confession were established, as were over 50 Protestant church schools[8]. Some of these communities that originally declared themselves to belong to the Augsburg Confession later transferred to the Helvetian

---

[8] These schools were owned by Protestant school boards created by the parents of the children enrolled in the schools. Later, the Protestant school boards and parish communities were merged into single bodies called Protestant parish boards. See "Odborny posudek o právním subjektu 'evangelická školní obec'" [Expert Opinion regarding the Legal Entity 'Protestant School Community'], *Revue církevního práva – Church Law Review,* 1(1995), 37-38.

Confession. Helvetian communities came to dominate the Czech Lands. In Moravia there were twice as many as their Augsburg counterparts, and in Bohemia there were five times as many Czech Helvetian communities as Augsburg communities.

The Orthodox had the same rights as Protestants, but they did not exercise them in the Czech Lands. During the toleration period no organization of Orthodox believers appeared in the Czech Lands, mainly because there were never more than scattered individuals who claimed to be Orthodox in this geographical region.

Alongside the undoubtedly positive meaning of the Acts of Toleration of Emperor Joseph II, their weaker side cannot be overlooked. They brought only partial liberation, and the toleration they established was inconsistent and insufficient. Several humiliating regulations were abolished only in 1848, and Protestants did not gain truly equal status until 1861.

The Status of Jews: Judenrecht

In contrast to Jewish law in the proper sense of the term, that is, the internal legal regulations of Jewish communities or the Jewish equivalent of canon law, the term "Jewish law" (*Judenrecht*) began to be used at the time of enlightened absolutism to designate state regulations that Jews were obliged to follow.

Toleration for Jews was extended by the edict of January 2, 1782, which followed the 1781 Act of Toleration. Other acts of toleration were issued for Moravian Jews (1782) and Silesian Jews (1781), and these were combined with the earlier regulations.

On August 3, 1797, Emperor Francis II issued the so-called "Jewish system" for Jews in Bohemia[9].

The Josephine Suppression of Religious Orders

Emperor Joseph II resolved to close down contemplative monasteries, which were, in the opinion of Enlightenment thinkers, not "useful," and to leave those religious houses dedicated to pastoral care, conducting schools, health care, and social welfare untouched. He started this suppression by issuing a legal regulation on November 29, 1781 that set up the legal framework for making violent advances against monasteries. On the basis of this act men and women religious houses were closed by

---

[9] Markéta LANDOVÁ, *Židovské právo [Jewish Law]*, Thesis: Faculty of Law, Charles University (Praha, 1997), p. 88.

the issuance of legal orders drawn up separately in each case. The remaining monasteries of a religious order were usually allowed to continue based on the *numerus clausus,* the number of members. In this way the transfer of religious from closed houses to the remaining house could not be made.

Religious priests from closed houses were urged to live alone; some of them accepted positions as pastors in the diocesan administration. Others made a livelihood as tutors or in similar employment. While lay brothers sometimes found positions as sacristans, the social arrangements for secularised women religious were much more complicated.

Not only subordinate officials, but the emperor himself also played an important role in the fact that the original aim of this law was often not achieved. Many times active religious houses, that is, "useful" houses, were closed, while on the other hand some contemplative monasteries which found favour in the eyes of the ruler were preserved. The determination of which monasteries would be suppressed and which preserved depended on the will and mood of the ruler and other state officials. In the end, at least half the monasteries and convents in the Czech Lands and Austrian Lands were closed. Some of them were restored at the end of the 19th century, some at the beginning of the 20th century, and some not until relatively recently.

The Foundation of Provincial Religious Funds: "Matice"

The property of closed monasteries, that is, communities of expelled men and women religious (often sold at prices far below market value) was not confiscated by the ruler, but turned over to separate property foundations. These foundations, or *matice,* were founded in 1782 and called Provincial Religious Funds. They had to supply benefices and church maintenance funds, because very few private individuals at this period were willing to donate funds for founding or maintaining new parishes. In Bohemia, some 250 new parishes were established due to the Provincial Religious Fund.

The harm arising from the liquidation of the majority of the monasteries was only partially compensated in this way. Violation of the personal freedom of the religious to live a consecrated life, which they had freely chosen, was also a great harm. So was the liquidation of their beneficial activity in social, educational, cultural, and economic fields. Unfair harm also arose from the sale of religious property for lower than fair market prices. As a result of the campaign of Joseph II against religious orders, landed property of the church in Bohemia and Moravia fell to less than half of its previous levels[10].

The Reform of Marriage Law and Procedural Law (1783-1811)

In the field of marriage law, Emperor Joseph II issued decree No. 117 on January 16, 1783, by which he cancelled the direct legal force of canon law and Jewish marriage law in the secular sphere. He left intact the church forms for entering into marriage contracts, but he withdrew marriage disputes from the competence of church courts and courts of the Jewish community, assigning them instead to secular courts.

Furthermore, the emperor cancelled the *privilegium fori* of clerics and priests. From that point on, clerics and rabbis were subject to the criminal jurisdiction of secular courts.

Imperial decree No. 946, the General Civil Code[11] was proclaimed on June 1, 1811, and went into effect on January 1, 1812. It remained in force in the Czech Lands until 1950. The text of the GCC was admirably prepared and it was not difficult to change or cancel its individual provisions. Amendments of marriage law in the GCC were passed in 1856, 1868, and 1919.

The marriage law contained in §§44-136 of the GCC followed the Josephine reform elaborated in the imperial decree of 1783. A characteristic mark of those enactments is the inclusion of large parts of canon law (for example, marriage impediments and separation from bed and board) and the liability of non-Catholics. This liability was an inference going beyond what was specified in canon law and ignoring the religious difference of non-Catholics by the absolutist state. Some of these excesses were eliminated in 1868, with another part removed in 1919.

In other matters of marriage law, however, the GCC took differences between Catholics and non-Catholics into consideration. Provision §111 did not allow divorce, but only for Catholics. It also applied, of course, when only one of the marriage partners was a Catholic. A special part of the GCC dealing with Jews (§§ 123-136) adopted several principles of Jewish law.

---

[10] Mojmír KALNÝ, *Církevní majetek a restituce [Church Property and Restitution]* (Praha: Občanský Insitut, 1995), p. 15.

[11] The following abbreviations will be used for subsequent references to legal codes and enumerations of laws:

GCC = General Civil Code
IC = Imperial Code
JLD = Journal of Laws and Decrees
JL = Journal of Laws

2.2 The Period of Transition (1848-1860)

The Revolution of 1848 and the Beginning of the Emancipation of Churches

Churches were liberated to a large extent from subordination to the state by the revolution of 1848. A more balanced arrangement of the relations between churches and the state began to be sought.

Professor Vratislav Bušek characterized this development with the following words: "Great slogans of civil rights promoted by the French Revolution called for constitutional guarantees and implementation in the Czech Lands. It was churches and religious societies who were in the front ranks of those who were thrilled by the freethinking slogans and demanded large autonomy and self-determination in their church and property affairs. Liberated from Josephinist oppression and state patronizing, they became privileged public-law corporations in the state, which the state sought to treat according to the principle of parity"[12].

Other religious freedoms were guaranteed in §§ 1-4 of imperial decree No. 151/1849 of the Imperial Code. By imperial decree No. 156/1850 of the IC, the autonomy of churches in the matter of clerical discipline was declared. Simultaneously, the *placet regium* was cancelled, so that the church could, from that time on, issue its own decrees without prior state approval. The church received the right to grant and cancel canonical missions and, in that way, to determine the appointment of professors of theology and teachers of religion. The church also received the right to confer the degree of Doctor of Theology.

On New Year's Eve of 1851, civil rights were suspended by decrees No. 2 and No. 3/1852 of the IC. Absolutism was re-established. By exception, the rights of churches and religious societies remained in effect.

The Concordat of 1855

As part of the gradual emancipation of the Catholic Church, the Austrian monarchy contracted an ambivalent international treaty with the Holy See for all its lands during the absolutist interlude, which it concluded on August 18, 1855. That agreement settled a series of unre-

---

[12] Vratislav BUŠEK, "Historický úvod do československého práva konfesního" [Historical Introduction to Czechoslovak State Ecclesiastical Law], in *Československé církevní zákony [Czechoslovak Church Laws]*, (Praha: Kompas, 1931), p. 21.

solved questions. The Catholic Church attained a larger degree of autonomy. The Church's independent decisions in the marriage disputes of
Catholics were recognized by the state. On the basis of article 10 of the
Concordat, the decree of October 8, 1856 suspended the provisions of
the GCC dealing with marriage law for Catholics. Once again, state
authorities had to observe canon law.

Some consequences of the Concordat can be appraised positively,
while others must be seen critically. While the Concordat helped the
emancipation of the Catholic Church, it damaged the beginnings of the
system of parity in two ways:

1) The Concordat contained formal assurance of the preservation of
   the "privileges" enjoyed by the Catholic Church up to that time.
2) More sensitive consequences stemmed from the control granted
   to Catholic authorities over common general schools. This control lasted 12 years and was cancelled by the enactment of Law
   No. 48/1868 of the IC, two years before the termination of the
   Concordat.

2.3 A Secular State: The Period of 1860-1918

The fall of Bach's absolutism after the defeat of the war over the Italian possessions (1859) caused extensive liberalization. The renewal of
constitutionalism was promised by the Diploma of October 1860. The
Constitution of February 1861 did not lay down civil rights, but progressively guaranteed freedom of religion with other laws. From 1860 to
1874, foundations were created for a secular state with a system of
church-state cooperation and parity for churches. It is possible to see an
inconsistency of this parity within the practices of the monarchy:

1) in the *ex officio* participation of several of the highest representatives of the Catholic Church in legislative assemblies, and
2) in the inability of the imperial family to give up pompous emphasis on Catholicism in life at court.

Emancipation of Protestants, the Protestant Decree of 1861

The improvement of the emancipation of Protestant churches, the first
steps of which were taken in the legislature of the years 1849-51, was
discussed at two conferences of provincial superintendents in Vienna in
1849 and 1859. These conferences resulted in the Protestant Decree

(imperial decree No. 41/1861 of the IC) by which "a complete equality of the rights of Protestants and other recognized denominations was brought about"[13].

The provisional constitution of the two Protestant churches, which was freely prepared by those churches, was issued as No. 42/1861 of the IC. The final version of the constitution, accepted by the general synods of those churches in 1864, was issued as No. 15/1866 of the IC.

Later, new church constitutions, accepted by general synods in the years 1889 and 1890 and issued in the IC in 1891, replace the above-mentioned constitutions. These new constitutions were further amended in 1900, 1905, and 1913.

Emancipation of the Orthodox Church in 1864

"Disunited" Greek Christians, who were at first recognized only in the Hungarian part of the monarchy, were recognized in the rest of the Habsburg lands in 1781. The Orthodox Church gained equality with the Catholic Church in the still undivided monarchy by law No. 91/1864 of the IC, and thereby acquired the more dignified name "Greek Eastern Church" throughout the empire.

Civil Rights Law (1867) and Subsequent Related Laws

On December 21, 1867, the constitutional law No. 142 of the IC on the common civil rights of citizens of the kingdoms and lands represented at the Imperial Council was enacted. It was called the December Constitution and was issued as part of the new constitution of the Cisleithan regions. This law contained many guarantees of freedom of religion in its articles 14-17. Article 16 regulated the private observance in the home of religions that were not legally recognized.

The constitutional enactment of constitutional principles of the freedom of religion was accomplished in Laws No. 47, 48, and 49/1868 of the IC on May 25, 1868, the so-called May Laws.

Law No. 47/1868 of the IC restored the force of the second heading of the GCC, and thereby restored the jurisdiction of secular courts for the marriage disputes of Catholics. A subsidiary civil form of marriage was established for the benefit of Catholics to whom church authorities denied entering into marriage contracts.

---

[13] BUŠEK, "Historický úvod," p. 25.

Law No. 48/1868 of the IC created new regulations governing the relation of churches to common schools. The Catholic Church's control was restricted to teaching catechism. Other churches and religious societies had equal rights as far as the teaching of their religion was concerned.

Law No. 49/1868 of the IC dealt with the inter-confessional relations of citizens. It governed the transfer of membership from one church to another and the church membership of children. It forbade the assessing of financial charges by a church to members of another church. In that way, this law established the condition of being nondenominational. According to the law, every citizen older than 14 could choose the church in which he wanted to be a member. The law revoked regulation § 768 of the GCC (1811), which stated that apostasy of Christianity was reason for disinheritance, and regulation § 122 of the Criminal Code (1852) on the punishable crime of inciting Christians to leave the faith.

Law No. 51/1870 of the IC concerning the marriage of persons not belonging to any recognized church or religious society strengthened their legal status and ordered state authorities to keep registers of their births, marriages, and deaths.

Termination of the Concordat

The Austro-Hungarian Empire withdrew from the Concordat of 1855 in July 1870 by the so-called Beust Dispatch. The justification for this move was that the other party – the Catholic Church – had "changed" because the First Vatican Council had declared the dogma of the infallibility of the pope. Law No. 50/1874 of the IC cancelled the Concordat in its entirety as a law of the Empire.

Law No. 50/1874 of the IC Concerning External Relations of the Catholic Church

This law was primarily concerned with the appointment to church offices and benefices, the exercise of church powers, patronage law, and property law. The law respected the autonomy of the church for internal affairs, but external affairs were governed in the first instance by state law, and church legislation had force only within the framework of state law. Church property enjoyed state protection, and decisions in property matters lay in the domain of state courts. Church administration was controlled by the state. Procurement of new financial means for the church, above all for the building of new parish churches and the remuneration of parish workers, were financed by the so-called "church concurrence," that is, the delineation of those who were charged and how they were charged for contribution.

Law No. 51/1874 of the IC Concerning Contributions to the Religious Fund

Recipients of benefices and religious orders were commanded to contribute to the religious fund from which poor parishes and monasteries were supported. This law created a kind of inner redistribution of property in the Catholic Church.

Provisional Law No. 47/1885 of the IC and Other Laws Concerning the Congrua

Congrua is a term of canon law designating support payments paid to clerics who were appointed to a church office. As a term of state ecclesiastical law, *congrua* was used to designate a supplementary payment from public sources in case *congrua* from church sources was not sufficient. In the Czech Lands, the institute of *congrua* from public sources was used to benefit several churches during the years 1885-1949. Other churches were supported by state subsidies that were sufficient to meet their needs.

Law No. 68/1874 of the IC Relating to the Recognition of Religious Societies

This law governed the recognition of churches and religious societies. If a church fulfilled the requirements of the law, it had the right to be recognized. The law did not lay down any *numerus clausus* for recognition. By that law, freedom of religion and the system of parity and coordination reached its peak in the Austro-Hungarian Empire. The Czechoslovak Republic later adopted that law.

Churches functioning in the territory of the Czech Lands were not, of course, forced to apply for recognition under the Law No. 68/1874 of the IC. They could organize according to different principles, combining common elements of an association and a foundation. This, for example, was the path chosen by the Free Reformed Church and the Baptist Union of the Brethren.

Emancipation of the Jewish Communities (1848, 1867, 1890)

Jewish emancipation began in 1848. There were many limitations, but already by the year 1859 these restrictions were withdrawn. Jewish communities had the right to keep their own registers of births, marriages, and deaths as other churches did, and they had the right to state subsidies. Constitutional Law No. 142/1867 of the IC accomplished full Jewish emancipation.

Special Law No. 57/1890 of the IC was issued to govern external relations of the Jewish religious society. It founded the legal status of Jewish communities up to 1949. The subsequent Law No. 9/1937 of the Journal of Laws and Decrees [JLD] concerning "the manner in which the Jewish religious society in Bohemia and Moravia is organized" never went into effect legally.

Recognition of Muslims

As a result of the annexation of Bosnia and Herzegovina in 1908, the Islamic religious society was legally recognized throughout the territory of the monarchy. This recognition was not accomplished by an administrative act, but by a special law in regard to the objective difference and legal specifics of that religion. This was Law No. 159/1912 of the IC, issued for the Cisleithan regions.

2.4 A Secular State: the Period 1918-1948

The Democratic Republic of 1918-1939

Churches and religious societies were liberated from state tutelage during the First Republic (1918-1938). In spite of initial displays of anti-Catholic sentiment, the measures for freedom of churches were much more favourable.

Church constitutions of non-Catholic churches were further integrated into the legal order of the state. The rules of canon law were recognized, too, in spite of several efforts by legal theorists to eliminate them from the public sphere.

The former legal regulation of church affairs was, in principle, adopted. But some obsolete measures from the Austrian regime, which restricted churches too much, were not applied. The initially proposed concept of separation of the churches from the state proved to be unacceptable.

Law No. 111/1919 of the JLD that amended provision § 303 of the Criminal Code with the offence of "abuse of clerical office in a political field" had a certain parallel with Bismarck's law from the period of the *Kulturkampf*. That provision, however, did not come into abuse in democratic Czechoslovakia.

The Catholic Church was more strongly affected by the Land Reform accomplished under Law No. 215/1919 of the JLD and its follow-up laws. Land Reform reduced land property of the church to 84% of what it had been before the Reform[14].

An excellent measure was Law No. 320/1919 of the JLD by which a choice between civil and church forms of marriage consent was enacted for all people in Czechoslovakia.

The Holy See recognized the new Czechoslovak state shortly after its inception, and this recognition was important for the international prestige of Czechoslovakia. By 1920 an embassy and a nunciature were established. Both archbishops in the Czech Lands were replaced, and bishops of Slovak nationality were appointed in all the dioceses of Slovakia.

Law No. 96/1925 of the JLD concerning inter-confessional relations was issued in 1925. In contrast to the law of 1868, the 1925 law raised the age limit for a free choice of religion from 14 to 16 years (§ 4).

The First Republic's Law Concerning Congrua

Law No. 122/1926 of the JLD set the minimum incomes (*congrua*) for clerics appointed to parish and other public church offices. If a cleric's income did not reach the limit, that cleric had the right to supplementary payments from the state up to that legal limit. Those churches and religious societies that were not integrated into the described system of *congrua* had the right to state subsidies determined proportionally according to the number of members. Therefore, churches and religious societies are divided into two categories: churches and religious societies who fit under the law concerning *congrua,* and those supported entirely by subsidies.

At times there were suggestions that the churches supported by subsidies were discriminated against within the system, but there does not seem to be any basis for discrimination. The fact itself that the amount of the subsidies was determined proportionally indicates strict justice in that matter.

---

[14] This 16% decrease represented a loss of 36,975 hectares. See KALNÝ, *Církevní majetek*, p. 16.

The modus vivendi *and the Subsequent Delimitation of Diocesan Borders*

The *modus vivendi* concluded between the Holy See and the Republic of Czechoslovakia was very short and modern for its time. It was in force from February 2, 1928. The agreement related especially to the procedure for the appointment of bishops in Czechoslovakia. The new delineation of diocesan borders following the state borders was realized in September 2, 1937 by the apostolic letter *Ad ecclesiastici regiminis incrementum.*

World War II and the 1945-48 Period

The fate of the Jewish communities in Czechoslovakia was especially tragic. After the holocaust (*Shoah*), the communities renewed their religious and social life to an extent that corresponded to the numbers who remained from the community. Only 10% of the pre-holocaust Czech Jewish community survived the *Shoah*. Moreover, only a fraction of the survivors came back to the country, and many of these stayed at home only for a time. The new regime did not deal with the Jewish communities fairly and did not return most of the property that had been confiscated by the Nazis. Some synagogues were destroyed by Nazis, while another substantial part remained in the hands of their new secular owners even after 1945, and a third part remained devoted to worship because it was turned over to the Czechoslovak Church. Post-war Jewish religious life was restored in only a few synagogues.

During the Nazi regime, beginning in March 1939, churches were the only institutions in the territory of the Protectorate of Bohemia and Moravia with inner freedom. Catholics participated in resistance to the Nazis. Many Catholics died in concentration camps or were executed. This sacrifice rehabilitated Catholics in the eyes of the nation.

Other churches participated in resistance to the Nazis as well, especially the Protestant Church of the Czech Brethren, which was connected with illegal groups of the YMCA, the prohibited Christian youth movement. The Union of the Brethren and the Czech Moravian Church (formerly, the Czechoslovak Church) were also persecuted. The Czech Orthodox Eparchy was liquidated for hiding Czechoslovak soldiers from Great Britain.

The result of the forced violent expulsion and resettlement of three million Germans after the war also proved to be negative in the religious field. The Catholic and Protestant pastoral church service weakened noticeably in the borderland. The loss of Sub-Carpathian Ruthenia and its one million inhabitants of high religiosity also weakened the position of the faithful in the post-war state, while the repatriation of Czechs from abroad strengthened some small churches.

Attacks Against Land Property of the Churches

During the 1945-48 period, the Communist Party steadily expanded its control of the state. The Revision of Land Reform was prepared as a part of the attack against property rights, but after the communist *coup d'état* in February, 1948 it was realized together with the New Land Reform. Both measures resulted in the liquidation of land property of the churches.

2.5 The Atheistic Ideological State: A Confessional State *à rebours* (1948-1989)

Beginnings of Persecution

As soon as the Communist Party came into power at the end of February 1948, it strengthened its dictatorship with legal and illegal steps. This combination of legal and illegal means was used noticeably to create new relations between churches and the state.

On May 9, 1948, the new constitution was adopted. That constitution declared several civil rights, including freedom of religion, but churches and religious societies were not mentioned in that constitution. The Communists were able to use restrictive measures of former legal regulations against churches and religious societies. Against the Catholic Church, for example, the regime used Law No. 50/1874 of the IC.

The provision on "the abuse of clerical office in a political field" was another rule that the Communists could use. The governing group was not pleased with that measure, however, and replaced it with other measures of the Criminal Code from Law No. 231/1948 of the Journal of Laws [JL] on the protection of the people's democratic republic. That law contained a draconian punishment of "subversive" activities. Hundreds of citizens, including many faithful and higher church representatives, were punished under that law during the time that it was in force. For example, because Catholic bishops were unwilling to subordinate the Catholic Church to the totalitarian Communist system, they were interned one by one.

New Laws on Churches and Religious Societies

On October 14, 1949, two laws strongly constricting churches and religious societies were issued. Through the first of these measures, Law No. 217/1949 of the JL, the State Office for Church Affairs was established. This office exercised a strict control over churches and religious societies until 1956, when it was discontinued and its jurisdiction was turned over to other state authorities.

The second of these laws, Law No.218 /1949 of the JL, dealt with the provisions of economical security provided by the states for churches and religious societies. In fact, this law was a harsh interference by the state. One of its provisions stated that a cleric could function in office only if he had received state approval, and that approval could be revoked at any time. State approval was also needed in the case of lay preachers. Strict control was accomplished by provisions of the Criminal Code punishing performance of pastoral service without state approval.

Liquidation of Religious Orders

All priories were attacked on the nights of April 13 and April 17, 1950. Religious men were interned in centralized camps for some months. Afterwards they were dispersed to prisons, forced labour camps, labour units of the Czechoslovak Army, and industrial labour units. The revival of the male orders was not allowed even during the Prague spring in 1968. Some of them worked in underground later, and they returned to the priories in 1990.

Parts of convents were later attacked in August 1950, and sisters were also interned in centralized camps. Later, all other convents were gradually liquidated and sisters had to change their job and work at factories or farms. No novices were allowed to enter to bring about the extinction of religious orders of sisters. Only in 1968, in the time of socialism "with a human face", were the orders permitted to admit a few novices, but they were not to return to the convents.

Other Persecutions

The Communist Party tried to force the Greek Catholic Church to join the Orthodox Church in 1950. However, a majority of priests and religious did not go over, nor did they obtain state approval for their ministries, and were deported with their families from Slovakia to Czech border territories. The whole Church was *via facti* dissolved, and was only restored in 1968. On the other hand, the Church of the Seventh Day

Adventists was prohibited by an explicit administrative act (1952-56). Protestant churches were also persecuted, especially the Protestant Church of the Czech Brethren and the Baptists. Lay activities in associations and periodicals were liquidated one by one.

2.6 Restoration of a Secular State after 1989

Legislation in the 1990-92 Period

At the end of the year 1989, provisions of the Criminal Code relating to religious activities were cancelled. Talks between representatives of the federal government and the Holy See, held from December 18 to December 20, 1989, resulted in the agreement that the *modus vivendi* was no longer in force.

The provision concerning the need of state approval for pastoral activities of clerics was rescinded in January 1990. Since then, the state has not intervened into the internal affairs of churches. The Charter of Fundamental Rights and Freedoms, a constitutional law, enacted the principle of non-interference of the state into church affairs a year later.

In 1990, diplomatic relations between Czechoslovakia and the Holy See were restored.

Churches and religious societies are still being supported by the state under Law No. 218/1949 of the JL. State subsidies have been paid directly to the head offices of churches since January 1, 1991, and not to individual clerics. Collections and donations are still an important financial source for churches, and these churches enjoy tax allowances.

170 religious houses were returned to religious orders by two laws passed during the 1990-91 period.

The Charter on Fundamental Rights and Freedoms, passed on January 9, 1991, laid down the foundations of the protection of human and civil rights. Freedom of religious was placed in articles 15 and 16. Article 16 states that churches and religious societies administer their own affairs. In particular, they establish authorities, appoint clerics, and establish religious and other institutions independently from the state.

Law No. 308/1991 of the JL, concerning freedom of religious faith and the status of churches and religious societies, followed the Charter. It was in force from September 1, 1991 until January 3, 2002. A list of 19 churches and religious societies acting in the territory of the Czech Republic was appended to the Law. For Slovakia, a list of 14 churches and religious societies was appended.

The law is divided into three parts. The first part states that everyone has the right to practice his religion alone or with others, to be nondenominational, to spread his or her faith, and not to be forced to practice any religion. Parents or tutors decide for children younger than 15 years of age. The second part deals with the legal status of churches and religious societies. The third part governs the registration of churches and religious societies. Church entities have the status of legal personalities according to church statutes.

Law No. 234/1992 of the JL amended the Family Law. By that amendment, the church form of marriage consent was approved, so that marriage contracted with the assistance of church authorities has legal force[15].

Legislation of the Independent Czech Republic since 1993

The Czechoslovak legal order was adopted by the new state, including the enactment that ratified and published international covenants on human rights and fundamental freedoms obliging the Czech Republic. The latter was immediately binding and had precedence over other laws. Before all it is *The International Agreement on Civil and Political Rights* from 1966.

Churches have founded over 130 church schools since 1990. There are five theological faculties in the Czech Republic. These faculties are integrated into public universities.

A decision of the Constitutional Court of the Czech Republic from March 26, 1997 rejects the jurisdiction of secular courts in the disputes dealing with the termination of a service relationship involving members of clergy. This judgment was made in accordance with the provision of the Charter of Fundamental Rights and Freedoms that churches administer their affairs independently, establish their own bodies of organization, and appoint their clergy separately from the State authority.

In 1994 pastoral service in prisons and in 1998 in the Czech Army was provided. The restitution of the Church property, however, is not yet fully realized, and a new system of the financing of Church has yet to be implemented.

---

[15] See Damián NĚMEC, "Příspěvek k diskusi o současné a budoucí sekulárněprávní úpravě uzavírání manželství ..." [A Contribution to the Discussion on the Secular Regulation of Contracting Marriage in the Present and Future], in *Revue církevního práva – Church Law Review,* 2(1995), 73-80, and Ignác HRDINA, "Kanonické uzavření manželství v českém právním řádu" [Canonical Contracting of Marriage in the Czech Legal Order], *Právník [The Jurist],* 5(1996),417-24.

Between 1999 and 2001 a new state ecclesiastical law was prepared. It was read in the Parliament several times, but was rejected by the Senate and vetoed by the President because of some restricting formulations. In spite of these facts, the House of Deputies confirmed the Law and it came into effect under number 3/2002 JL on January 7, 2002.

BONUM CONIUGUM
FROM A SOCIO-CULTURAL PERSPECTIVE

AUGUSTINE MENDONÇA

INTRODUCTION

There is no doubt that the refreshing doctrinal and pastoral insights provided by the Second Vatican Council in its pastoral constitution on the Church in the modern world, *Gaudium et spes*[1], has been a veritable source of positive developments in our understanding of the theological and juridical nature of marriage. This particular issue alone, that is, marriage, has inspired volumes of literature in theology, canon law and other human sciences. In explaining the nature of this constitution, the council fathers made extra efforts to explain that the teaching of *Gaudium spes* had two essential dimensions: doctrinal and pastoral. In the *Notae* attached to the introductory segment of the document, the council emphasised that the two parts of the documents were intrinsically linked. The document carried the qualification "pastoral" because it intended to express the Church's relationship to the world and modern people in light of the doctrinal principles proclaimed in it. The first part, therefore, would explicate the doctrinal principles related to the human being, the world in which human beings live and the Church's relationship to them. In the second part, the document would focus on the pressing current problems the world was facing and the Church's response to them. The council fathers went on to stress that this constitution must be read and understood in accord with the general principles of theological interpretation taking into account the changing aspects of those problems[2].

---

[1] SECOND VATICAN COUNCIL, Pastoral Constitution on the Church in the Modern World, *Gaudium et spes (=GS)*, 7 December 1965, in *Acta Apostolicae Sedis (=AAS)*, 58 (1966), pp. 1025-1120; English translation in Austin FLANNERY (Gen. Ed.), Vatican Council II, Vol. 1, *The Conciliar and Postconciliar Documents* (=FLANNERY I), New rev. ed., Northport, NY, Costello Publishing Company; Dublin, Dominican Publications, 1996, pp. 903-1001. Because of inaccuracy in translation of some important technical terms presented in the original Latin text, we will try to adapt Flannery's translation where we consider it necessary.

[2] See *Acta synodalia Sacrosancti Concilii Oecumenici Vaticani II (=Acta synodalia)*, In Civitate Vaticana, Typis polyglottis Vaticanis, 1970-1978, vol. IV, pars VII, p. 734.

And any effort on the part of canonists to determine the juridical relevance of any doctrinal-pastoral statements made in the constitution cannot overlook these fundamental postulates clearly implied in it.

In his apostolic constitution promulgating the new Code of Canon Law, *Sacrae disciplinae leges*, Pope John Paul II stated: "This instrument which the Code is fully corresponds to the nature of the Church, especially as it is proposed by the teaching of the Second Vatican Council in general and in a particular way by its ecclesiological teaching. Indeed, in a certain sense this new Code could be understood as a great effort to translate this same conciliar doctrine and ecclesiology in *canonical* language. If, however, it is impossible to translate perfectly into *canonical* language the conciliar image of the Church, nevertheless the Code must always be referred to this image as the primary pattern whose outline the Code ought to express insofar as it can by its very nature"[3]. This statement of the Holy Father clearly suggests that a proper methodology for interpreting the norms laid out in the new Code must take into account the conciliar insights. This, I believe, is particularly true in matters pertinent to matrimonial legislation.

It is now universally recognised by both theologians and canonists that the Second Vatican Council adopted a truly personalist view of marriage. In presenting its understanding of marriage from a natural and redeemed perspective, the council refrained from approaching marriage solely from an institutional viewpoint. It saw marriage as an "intimate community of life and conjugal love." Beyond its procreative finality, the council admitted the good of the spouses, an aspect sorely overlooked, or rather deliberately excluded prior to the council from the juridical conception of marriage. In other words, for the council, marriage was not purely an institution for the procreation of offspring but also meant for the mutual "perfection" of the spouses. It is this new aspect of marriage that is the focus of this study.

Because marriage is a natural reality, it cannot be fully understood and appreciated outside the concrete cultural context in which it is lived out and nurtured. This is particularly true of the "*bonum coniugum.*" What the good of spouses is can be determined only in light of the culture of a given people. Whether this good of marriage is an essential

---

[3] See JOHN PAUL II, Apostolic Constitution, *Sacrae disciplinae leges*, in *AAS*, 75 (1983-II), p. XI; English translation in *Code of Canon Law*, Latin-English trans. prepared under the auspices of the Canon Law Society of America, Washington, DC, Canon Law Society of America, 1999, p. xxx.

element or a property, an institutional or personalistic end, one can no longer relegate it to the status of a juridically irrelevant "secondary end." It is now an aspect of marriage which deserves at least equal, if not greater, recognition in comparison to the good of offspring which alone dominated canonical jurisprudence on the object of matrimonial consent.

The principal hypothesis of this study is that the concept of *bonum coniugum* is an intrinsic essential aspect of marriage which, like marriage itself, is culturally defined. As an end, it is certainly extrinsic to marriage, but as an end, it becomes, together with *bonum prolis*, the object of the marital covenant or consent (marriage *in fieri*) as proclaimed by both the conciliar document *Gaudium et spes* and the new codes.

This study will be divided into five sections to demonstrate the validity of the hypothesis. First, marriage will be examined from a cultural perspective. For the sake of brevity, we will limit our reflections to the Church's approach to culture and culture's influence on the understanding of *bonum coniugum*. Second, because the introduction of the concept of *bonum coniugum* into canonical legislation is an innovation, it would be helpful to review in a summary fashion the conciliar teaching on it, and this will be done in the second section. Third, the council acknowledged an intrinsic link between *bonum coniugum* and conjugal love. Any treatment of *bonum coniugum* would certainly be incomplete without analysing the relationship between the two. The third section, therefore, will focus on the juridic relevance of conjugal love and *bonum coniugum*. Fourth, the concept of *bonum coniugum* has received inquisitive attention from both theologians and canonists, who have examined the concept from different perspectives. Therefore, the fourth section will consider the meaning of *bonum coniugum* according to current canonical doctrine and jurisprudence. Fifth, generally Rotal sentences provide new insights into the applicability of freshly enacted legal norms to concrete cases, and those insights serve as the foundation for the development of canonical jurisprudence on issues of the kind we are dealing with in this study. Therefore, a few selected Rotal sentences will be reviewed in order to determine how the concept of *bonum coniugum* has been handled at the Rota.

1. MARRIAGE AS A CULTURAL REALITY

Culture may be regarded as the soul of a community. It is a dynamic force which shapes and moulds the life-style, thought patterns and behaviour of the people belonging to a particular community. It is culture that produces in people characteristics which become marks of identification of a community as a whole and of its members in particular.

The complex nature of culture defies any uniform definition. The Second Vatican Council acknowledged this problem when it said that "culture necessarily has historical and social overtones, and the word 'culture' often carries with it sociological and ethnological connotations; in this sense one can speak about a plurality of cultures"[4]. In whatever terms culture may be defined, there is no doubt that culture as a dynamic and vital force, which shapes and directs the life-style of a particular community, invariably influences human personality and behaviour.

In order to have a proper understanding and appreciation of the meaning and influences of culture on human behaviour, one should view it from its static and dynamic perspectives. As a static reality, culture embodies knowledge, beliefs, morals, law, customs, opinions, religion, superstition, art, etc., a distinctive heritage of a particular community[5]. In its dynamic aspect, culture is an ever-changing reality which shapes the life of a particular community; it evolves, it acts and is acted upon by the common experiences of its members. It changes the people's way of life and is capable of being changed. In this aspect, culture has been described as the "sum total of the attainments and learned behaviour patterns of any specific period, race, people, regarded as expressing traditional way of life subject to gradual but continuous modification by succeeding generations." Or, it is the "the act of developing by education, discipline, social experience; the training or refining of the moral and intellectual faculties." Or again, it is "the training, development, or strengthening of the powers, mental or physical, or the condition thus produced; improvement or refinement of mind, morals and tastes; enlightenment or civilisation"[6]. Or, "an ordered system of meaning and of symbols in terms of which social interaction takes place"; it is "the fabric of meaning in terms of which human beings interpret their

---

[4] *GS* 53.

[5] See *Webster's Third New International Dictionary of English Language,* unabridged ed., by Philip Babcock Gove, and Merriam-Webster editorial staff, Springfield, MA, G. & C. Merriam, 1981, p. 552; *Funk & Wagnalls New Standard Dictionary of the English Language,* Isaac K. FUNK [editor in chief], New York, Funk and Wagnalls, 1923, p. 629.

[6] See *Webster's Third New International Dictionary of the English Language*, p. 552; *Funk & Wagnalls New Standard Dictionary of the English Language*, p. 629.

experiences and guide their action"[7]. Even the Second Vatican Council spoke of culture in this sense while referring to it as "all those things which go to refining and developing of diverse mental and physical endowments of the human person"[8].

Each culture has its own unique way of communicating information and knowledge to the members of a particular group. This communication is carried out through the use of distinct tools, symbols, language, as well as systems of abstract thought which, through the process of assimilation and incorporation, influence and even direct people's life-activities. In other words, cultural forces play an important role in the functional aspects of personality of the members of a particular cultural group[9].

As far as the specific influences of culture on human mind and personality are concerned, psychological studies indicate that one's perception, cognition, emotion, motivation and socialisation certainly bear the culture's unique stamp. Cross-cultural studies also confirm that the manner in which people of different cultures perceive subjective and objective events are learned, therefore, ecologically (culturally) determined[10]. Again, all these insights support the view that culture exerts significant influence on the different aspects of human personality.

Marriage is a natural human reality. Its very existence and purpose are determined by human nature itself. The naturalness of marriage is founded on the sexually distinct nature of human beings, that is, in their "maleness" and "femaleness," oriented toward its intrinsic ends. This truth has been revealed in the creation story: "God created the human being in the image of himself, in the image of God he created the human being, *male* and *female* he created them" (Gen. 1:27). This "maleness" and the "femaleness" of the human beings is designed by God for the mutual fulfilment or complementarity of the spouses: "It is not good that the man should be alone. I will make him a helpmate" (Gen. 2:18), and for the generation of new life: "Be fruitful and multiply, fill the earth and conquer it" (Gen. 1:28). These biblical references constitute the foundation of the Church's teaching on marriage and family.

[7] See Clifford GEERTZ, *The Interpretation of Cultures*, New York, Basic Books, 1973, pp 144-145.

[8] *GS* 53.

[9] See Gustav JAHODA, "The Colour of a Chameleon: Perspective on Concepts of 'Culture'," in *Cultural Dynamics*, 6, 3 (1993), p. 281.

[10] See D. MOTET, art., "Cross-Cultural Psychology," in *Baker Encyclopedia of Psychology*, ed. by David G. BENNER, Grand Rapids, MI, Baker Book House, 1985, p. 265.

Two favourite topics of Pope John Paul II's teachings, and he never fails to include relevant conciliar reflections on the matter, have been marriage and family. He has always spoken eloquently on these two themes. The relationship between culture and marriage/family has been a frequent object of his exhortations, homilies and allocutions. For example, in his post-synodal apostolic exhortation, *Familiaris consortio*, of 22 November 1981, he said: "Since God's plan for marriage and family touches men and women in the concreteness of their daily existence in specific social and cultural situations, the Church ought to apply herself to understanding the situations within which marriage and family are lived today, in order to fulfil her task of serving"[11]. Again in his allocution to the Roman Rota in 1991, he said: "Precisely because it is a reality that is deeply rooted in human nature itself, marriage is affected by the cultural and historical conditions of every people. They have left their mark upon the institution of marriage. The Church, therefore, cannot prescind from the cultural milieu."[12] He reaffirmed the natural character of marriage in his recent allocution of 1 February 2001 saying: "The ecclesiastical Magisterium and the canonical legislation contain abundant references to the natural character of marriage. In *Gaudium et spes*, the Second Vatican Council, after stating that 'God himself is the author of marriage, which is endowed with various goods and ends' (no. 48), tackles some problems of conjugal morality by referring to 'objective criteria, which are founded in the very nature of the human person and of his/her actions' (no. 51)"[13].

Because marriage is rooted in human nature, the inner structure and external manifestation of marriage are inevitably influenced by cultural forces. Even the notion of a Christian marriage, although based on

---

[11] JOHN PAUL II, Apostolic Exhortation, *Familiaris consortio (=FC)*, 22 November 1981, in Austin FLANNERY (Gen. Ed.), *Vatican Council II*, Vol. 2, *More Postconciliar Documents* (=FLANNERY II), New Revised Edition, Northport, NY, Costello Publishing Company; Dublin, Dominican Publications, 1998, p. 817.

[12] See JOHN PAUL II, Allocution to the Roman Rota, 28 January 1991, in *AAS*, 83 (1991), pp. 947-953; English translation in William H. WOESTMAN (ed.), *Papal Allocutions to the Roman Rota, 1939-1994*, Ottawa, ON, Saint Paul University, Faculty of Canon Law, 1994, pp. 214-218, here at pp. 214-215.

[13] JOHN PAUL II, Allocution to the Roman Rota, 1 February 2001, in *L'Osservatore romano*, 2 February 2001, p. 7: "Il Magistero ecclesiastico e la legislazione canonica contengono abbondanti riferimenti all'indole naturale del matrimonio. Il Concilio Vaticano II, nella Gaudium et spes, premesso che 'Dio stesso è l'autore del matrimonio, dotato di molteplici beni e fini' (n. 48), affronta alcuni problemi di moralità conjugale rifacendosi a 'criteri oggettivi, che hanno il loro fondamento nella natura stessa della persona umana e dei suoi atti' (n. 51)."

Gospel values, because marriage is first and foremost a natural reality, cannot be formulated outside the context of a particular culture. And because cultures differ one from another, the object of marital content would also differ from culture to culture. For example, in the Western culture marriage is seen predominantly as an agreement between two individuals, namely the spouses. Parental role is practically insignificant in such an agreement. It is the consent of the parties alone that brings marriage into being. Furthermore, in the western culture, marriage is the culmination of the love two persons have for each other at the time of exchanging marital consent. And this mutual love would naturally be oriented toward the good of the spouses[14]. But this is not the situation in African, Asian and other societies. Writing specifically on marriage among the Igbo people of Nigeria, for example, B. Okonkwor explains that "In Igbo traditional society, marriage is a social rather than a private affair, uniting two families as well as individuals"[15]. In a similar vein, Nguyên Thê Viên writes the following on the Vietnamese tradition on the institution of marriage: "The Vietnamese marriage is controlled by a plethora of customs, traditions and laws in which individual's significance, freedom and feelings pale in comparison to the nation's and clan's very existence"[16]. He continues: "The purpose of Vietnamese marriage is to serve and worship ancestors, and to bring children into the world in order to continue the species. Therefore, marriage is not a matter between two individuals but that of the whole family, even the whole clan"[17]. The same familial and communitarian view of marriage is prevalent also in countries of the Indian subcontinent[18]. A similar approach is prevalent in these cultures in regard to the importance of conjugal love. Marriage in these cultures is regarded as a "school of love" rather than a "result of love." Okonkwor explains that "love"

---

[14] See Lawrence G. WRENN, "Refining the Essence of Marriage," in his *The Invalid Marriage,* Washington, DC, Canon Law Society of America, 1998, pp. 202-218.

[15] Belonwu H. OKONKWOR, *The Role of Matrimonial Consent in Igbo Traditional Marriage in the Light of the New Canonical Legislations: A Comparative Study,* JCD diss., Rome, Pontificia Universitas Urbaniana, 1985, p. 19.

[16] Nguyên THE VIEN, *The Traditional Role of Parents or Guardians in Vietnamese Marriages and Canonical Freedom of Consent,* JCL thesis, Washington, DC, The Catholic University of America, 1994, p. 42.

[17] Ibid., p. 43.

[18] For a comprehensive study of this particular issue, see Augustine MENDONÇA, "The Importance of Considering Cultural Contexts in Adjudicating Marriage Nullity Cases, With Special Reference to South East Asian Countries," in *Philippiniana sacra,* 31 (1996), pp. 189-268, especially pp. 206-221.

plays very little influence on a prospective marriage. He says that it may be hard for the people of the western world to appreciate the positive attitude of the Igbo people to the arranged marriage or the notable influence of parents in their children's marriage; particularly due to the fact of the apparent lack of love or romantic love in the system. Really, sentimental love has no room in Igbo or in fact, in African marriage custom. In other words, "love, then, usually has no part to play in native courtship. Later a substitute for love may develop consisting of a certain amount of affection or favour bestowed by the husband upon his wife"[19]. In this scenario, the good of the spouses, although not explicitly excluded from married life, may not have the same relevance it has in the western culture.

What is important to note in these examples are the real cultural differences in matters which pertain to the very nature of marriage, its contents and finality. Marriage is certainly not perceived and lived out in identically the same way by all societies. John Paul II explicitly alluded to this point in his address to Rotal officials on 22 January 1996. He said: "However, for a suitable judgement in their regard, I consider it no less important to recall a few points about the need to evaluate and weigh every individual case, taking into account the *individuality of the subject* as well as the *particular nature of the culture* in which he/she grew up and lives"[20]. He added, "Thus your most sensitive judicial function is situated and in some ways channelled in the age-old effort by which the Church, from her contact with the cultures of every time and place, has adopted whatever she found that was basically valid and suitable to the immutable requirements of the dignity of humans, made in the image of God"[21].

As observed above, culture not only influences people's lives but also is being impacted upon by the newly emerging trends in every society. This is quite evident in the unprecedented changes we are presently witnessing in our traditional values and institutions. These changes have been accelerated by the runway advances made by medical, biological, genetic and technological sciences, which seriously challenge every value traditionally cherished by the human family, including marriage and family, the most fundamental pillars or cornerstones of every society.

[19] See OKONKWOR, *The Role of Matrimonial Consent in Igbo Traditional Marriage*, p. 24.
[20] See JOHN PAUL II, Allocution to the Roman Rota, 22 January 1996, in *L'Osservatore romano*, Weekly English language edition, 31 January 1996, p. 5.
[21] Ibid.

A few years ago, reflecting on the erosion of family life by the forces of modern secular culture, Jonathan Sacks, the chief Rabbi of the United Hebrew Congregations of the British Commonwealth, said: "The family is where we acquire the skills and language of relationship. It is where we learn to handle the inevitable conflicts within any human group. It is where we first take the risk of giving and receiving love. Of all the influences upon us, the family is by far the most powerful. Its effects stay with us for a lifetime. It is where one generation passes on its values to the next and ensures the continuity of a civilisation. For any society, the family is the crucible of its future"[22]. Sacks went on to explain how this channel of values has become a victim of the secular culture sweeping across our modern world.

The impact of culture on marriage and family life has been a constant concern of the Church. In the introductory statement of *Gaudium et spes*, we read the following observation of the council fathers: "Ours is a new age of history with critical and swift upheavals spreading gradually to all corners of the earth. They are products of man's intelligence and creative activity, but they recoil upon him, upon his judgements and desires, both individual and collective, upon his ways of thinking and acting in regard to people and things. We are entitled then to speak of a real social and cultural transformation whose repercussions are felt too on the religious levels"[23]. Following this statement, the council went on to explain some of the rapidly changing values, attitudes, morals, religion, etc. This concern of the council clearly underlines the effect of culture on human life and human behaviour.

In his allocution of 1 February 2001, John Paul II says: "Among the more serious challenges which the Church faces today is the all pervading individualistic culture, which tends [...] to circumscribe and limit marriage and family to the world of the private"[24].

A fact no one can deny is that the socio-cultural ethos we live in continues to experience unprecedented and rapid changes which deeply affect our values, beliefs, life-style and behaviour. This phenomenon is

---

[22] See Jonathan SACKS, "The heart of our moral crisis: Erosion of the family is widespread but its demise is not at all inevitable," in *The Ottawa Citizen*, Friday, 31 March 1995, p. A11. This essay of Sacks was based on extracts from his book: *Faith in the Future*.

[23] *GS* 4; FLANNERY I, p. 905.

[24] JOHN PAUL II, Allocution to the Roman Rota, 1 February 2001, p. 7: "Tra le più ardue sfide che attendono oggi la Chiesa vi è quella di un'invadente cultura individualistica, tendente, [...], a circomscrivere e confinare il matrimonio e la famiglia nel mondo del privato."

not without its effect on how people perceive, think and decide on matters that are important to personal and community life. For example, a study published in 1992 identified several mentalities, such as "anti-commitment mentality," "contraceptive mentality," "divorce mentality," etc., the direct results of cultural changes, that are presently sweeping across the western culture, which could seriously affect marital consent[25]. This is not solely a western phenomenon because other cultures are also going through similar transformations, which in turn are likely to exert their influence on matrimonial consent and married and family life.

From the above reflections we may make the following summary observations: First, marriage is a natural reality which expresses itself externally in culturally defined forms. Second, because cultures differ from one another, the structures and values which express the reality of marriage would necessarily vary. Third, because culture is a changeable reality, marriage, being a culturally conditioned institution, is also subject to changes experienced by a given culture. Therefore, a proper understanding of marriage and a just and equitable interpretation of any legal norm pertinent to it must necessarily take into consideration all the vicissitudes of a given culture in which marriage is celebrated and family life nurtured.

2. CONCILIAR AND PAPAL TEACHING ON *BONUM CONIUGUM*

The theological and pastoral insights provided by the council in *Gaudium et spes* on marriage continue to generate lively discussion in canonical circles. As mentioned in the introduction, the conciliar teaching provided the foundation for most of the fundamental concepts and norms presented in the new Codes. The concept of *"bonum coniugum,"* no doubt, is one such concept taken directly from *Gaudium et spes*. What did the council fathers really say about this concept?

The expression *"bonum coniugum"* occurs only once in articles 47-52 of the constitution. And this is found in art. 48: "[...] in view of the *good both of the spouses* and children, and of the society this sacred bond no longer depends on human decision alone"[26]. This statement clearly

---

[25] See I. GRAMUNT - L.A. WAUCK, "'Lack of Due Discretion': Incapacity or Error," in *Ius canonicum*, 32 (1992), pp. 533-558, especially pp. 551-554.

[26] "hoc vinculum sacrum intuitu boni, tum coniugum et prolis tum societatis, ex humano arbitrio non pendet" (*GS* 48).

implies that the "good of the spouses" is an intrinsic aspect of the sacred bond, which is marriage. Having said this, the constitution deliberately refrains from providing any further elaboration on the nature of this good. It does not explicitly say anywhere, for example, if this *bonum* is an essential element, an end, or a good in the augustinian sense. Avoidance of any technical explanations is certainly in conformity with the nature of the constitution as a pastoral statement rather than as a juridical proclamation. The council had no intention of engaging in a dialogue with the world in technical terms. It deliberately chose to use simple terminology intelligible to ordinary people. But this approach had not been without serious consequences for interpretation. For example, the term *bonum* alone has been used several times in different combinations with meanings ranging from the specifically technical to the more generic[27]. And yet there can be no doubt that it was the council's mind that the good of the spouses was to be an essential aspect of the institution of marriage. The council made no definitive determination on whether this good is an end, a property or an element. Therefore, the expression "ordered to the good of the spouses" is not found in *Gaudium et spes* while "ordered to the good of offspring" has been stated twice in the document[28]. This does not mean, however, that a proper interpretation of the conciliar teaching cannot lead to the conclusion that the marriage covenant or marriage itself is ordered to the good of the spouses[29]. After all, this is exactly what both Code Commissions thought when they drafted c. 1055, §1 (CCEO c. 776, §1).

In one of his more recent sentences, Burke notes that "the term 'good of the spouses' – *bonum coniugum* – has practically no precedent in

---

[27] See Charles J. SCICLUNA, *The Essential Defintion of Marriage According to the 1917 and 1983 Codes of Canon Law: An Exegetical and Comparative Study*, Lanham, London, New York, University Press of America, 1995, p. 174. Here Sciculna enumerates the following instances where the term *bonum* has been used with differing meanings: *bonum coniugum* (48a); *bonum liberorum [prolis]* (48a, 50b, c); *bonum parentum* (50a, b); *bonum fidei* (51a); *bona matrimonii et familiae* (52e, d); *bonum totius personae* (49a); *bonum communitatis familiaris* (50b); *bonum societatis [temporalis]* (48a, 50b); *bonum Ecclesiae* (50b).

[28] See *GS* 48 and 50.

[29] See BURKE, "Progressive Jurisprudential Thinking," p. 470, where the author argues "*nowhere in the council documents is it presented as an end.*" Citing his article of 1989, he reiterates again on the same page that "*Gaudium et spes* 'nowhere says that marriage is ordered to the good of the spouses'." While technically Burke is correct, because the council does not say that marriage is ordered to *bonum coniugum*, it seems abundantly clear to me in the context of *GS* 48-52. One can certainly claim that it is implicit in the conciliar teaching on marriage.

theological or canonical doctrine, to express an end of marriage"[30]. This observation of Burke is partly correct because, as stated above, not even the constitution *Gaudium et spes* spoke explicitly of *bonum coniugum* as an end of marriage. I say "partly" correct because the traditional Catholic doctrine underlying the nature of marriage has always at least *implicitly*, admitted the principle that marriage is of its very nature ordered to this good just as it is ordered to the good of offspring. The very concept, I believe, is rooted in the Scriptures and in canonical tradition[31].

The 1917 Code certainly had a very limited view of the nature and elements of marriage. It did not contain any formal definition of marriage as the present Code does in canon 1055, §1 (CCEO c. 776, §1), nor did it explicitly endorse the augustinian *bona*. In canon 1013, §1 of the 1917 Code, there was explicit recognition of two ends of marriage: first, the procreation and education as its primary end, and second, "mutual help and remedy of concupiscence" as the secondary end. This secondary end, which could have been elaborated into the juridical concept of "*bonum coniugum*," apparently received no recognition within the context of the formal object of consent under the old code regime. The formal object of consent was the exclusive and perpetual right to the body for acts (sexual intercourse) per se suitable for the procreation of children (canon 1081, §2). Thus the emphasis was exclusively on the right to sexual intercourse open to procreation, the purely biological aspects of conjugal duty. The secondary end of "mutual help" and "remedy of concupiscence," which may be regarded with appropriate scientific analysis, the equivalent of the present expression "good of the spouses" (*bonum coniugum*), received little juridical consideration.

The magisterial teaching, however, derived principally from revelation contained in the bible, has been fairly consistent in referring to the "good of the spouses," although not with the same rich symbolism attributed to it by the conciliar statements. For example, we find direct

---

[30] Decision *c.* BURKE, 26 March 1998, in *ME*, 124 (1999), p. 239. In his latest article on this point Burke reiterates the same statement: "It is curious to find that this particular term has practically no precedent in theological or canonical writings, to express an end of marriage. [...]. The 1983 code is the first magisterial document where the *bonum coniugum* is used to express one of the ends of marriage." See Cormac BURKE, "Progressive Jurisprudential Thinking," in *The Jurist*, 58 (1998), p. 443.

[31] For a brief historical overview of the notion of *bonum coniugum*, see Enrica MONTAGNA, "*Bonum coniugum*: profili storici," in *Il "bonum coniugum" nel matrimonio canonico*, Studi giuridici XL, Città del Vaticano, Libreria editrice Vaticana, 1996, pp. 33-61.

recognition of the good of spouses as an element of marriage in Pius XI's encyclical *Casti connubii*, where he says:

> This outward expression of love in the home demands not only mutual help but must go further; it must have as its *primary purpose* that man and wife help each other day by day in *forming* and *perfecting* themselves in the *interior life*, so that through their partnership in life they may advance even more and more in virtue, and above all that they may grow in true love towards God and their neighbour, on which indeed "depends the whole Law of the Prophets"[32].

The good of the spouses consists in their personal perfection, namely in their interior life (emotional and psychological integration), in their spiritual life (growth in their personal relationship with God), and finally in social life (extension of their personal integration to the society). This personal and interpersonal growth or perfection of the spouses, Pius XI maintains, is the "primary cause and reason of marriage":

> This mutual interior formation of the spouses, this serious effort to perfect each other, can in all truth be said to be as the Roman Catechism teaches, the *primary cause and reason* for marriage, if marriage is to be considered not in the stricter sense as an institution for the procreation and education of offspring, but in a wider meaning of a communion of every aspect of life, a community, a society[33].

Even though the significance and intent of *Casti connubii* were more pastoral, moral and doctrinal, it may not be unreasonable to suggest that the foundation for later juridical recognition of *bonum coniugum* was already present in it.

Pope Pius XII, in his allocution of 29 October 1951 to the Italian Catholic Union of Midwives, while strongly reaffirming the subordinate position of the secondary ends of marriage (good of the spouses), stressed the importance of the "personal values" of marriage. He said that we must not "reject or belittle all that is good and right in the personal values deriving from matrimony and its consummation"[34]. Furthermore, to "reduce the communal life and man and woman and their marital relations to nothing more than an organic function for trans-mitting life-germs would be to convert the home, this sanctuary of the family, into a mere biological laboratory. The marital act, in its natural

---

[32] See PIUS XI, Encyclical letter *Casti connubii*, 31 December 1930, in *AAS*, 22 (1930), pp. 539-592, here at pp. 547-548 (emphasis added).

[33] Ibid., pp. 548-549 (emphasis added).

[34] See *AAS*, 43 (1951), pp. 835-854. English translation, in *Clergy Review*, 36 (1951), pp. 379-391 and 37 (1952), pp. 45-51, here at pp. 46-47.

structure, is a personal action, a simultaneous and direct co-operation of husband and wife which, because of the very nature of the agents and the distinctive character of the act, is the expression of the mutual self-giving that, in the words of Scripture, makes them 'one flesh'"[35]. And "these personal values, whether they belong to the order of the body and the senses or to that of the spirit, are real indeed and genuine, but that the Creator has set them in the second rank of the scale, not the first"[36].

Although Pius XII spoke highly of the *bonum coniugum* in his theological and pastoral reflections on marriage, as D. Fellhauer points out, his teaching as a whole constituted "a powerful reaffirmation of the position which saw in the *finis primarius* the 'exclusively determining factor' in canonical marriage, its sole *elementum iuridicum specificum*." In other words, despite Pius XII's emphasis on the personal-conjugal dimension, the concept of *bonum coniugum* remained in essence devoid of practical juridical value[37].

In his well-known encyclical letter, *Humanae vitae*, of 25 July 1968, Pope Paul VI echoed the conciliar teaching on marriage when he declared: "As a consequence, husband and wife, *through their mutual gift of themselves*, which is specific and exclusive to them alone, *seek to develop that kind of personal union in which they complement one another* in order to co-operate with God in the generation and education of new lives"[38].

The apostolic exhortation *Familiaris consortio* of Pope John Paul II also emphasised the fact that the conjugal union is dependent upon the equal dignity and responsibility of spouses, and the moral criterion for the authenticity of their relationship is the measure in which they can *achieve their personal fulfilment* in genuine self-giving[39].

The new *Catechism*, no. 2249, repeats this conciliar and magisterial teaching. In it we read: "The conjugal community is established upon the covenant and consent of the spouses. Marriage and family are ordered to the *good of the spouses*, to the procreation and the education of children." And again in no. 2363 the same teaching reappears:

---

[35] *Clergy Review*, 37 (1952), pp. 47-48.

[36] See ibid., p. 48.

[37] See David E. FELLHAUER, "The *Consortium omnis vitae* as a Juridical Element of Marriage," in *Studia canonica*, 13 (1979), pp. 99.

[38] See PAUL VI, Encyclical letter on the regulation of births, *Humanae vitae (=HV)* 8, in *AAS*, 60 (1968), pp. 481-503; English translation in FLANNERY II, pp. 397-416, here at p. 400.

[39] *FC* 22 (emphasis added).

"The spouses' union achieves the twofold end of marriage: the *good of the spouses* themselves, and the transmission of life. These two meanings or values of marriage cannot be separated without altering the couple's spiritual life and compromising the goods of marriage and the future of the family." With its introduction into the new *Catechism*, the expression *bonum coniugum* "cannot be treated as a merely canonical term, but has passed into general magisterial teaching and offers itself as a notion of considerable theological interest"[40].

In his Rotal allocution of 1 February 2001, John Paul II more than once reiterates the ordination of marriage covenant or of marriage itself to the good of the spouses and to the good of offspring. For example, he says: "In their turn, both codes promulgated by me, in formulating the definition of marriage, affirm that the '*consortium totius vitae*' is 'of its very nature ordered to the good of the spouses and to the generation and education of children."[41] Again he says: "The ordination to natural ends of marriage – the good of the spouses and procreation and education of offspring – is intrinsically present in the masculinity and femininity. This teleological nature is decisive for understanding the natural dimension of the union. In this sense, the natural character of marriage is better understood when it is not separated from the family. Marriage and family are inseparable, because the masculinity and femininity of the spouses are, of their very constitution, open to the gift of children. Without this opening there can be no good of the spouses worthy of its name"[42].

What we see here is an evolution in the Church's understanding of the theological nature of marriage, and in particular, of the good of the spouses (*bonum coniugum*). The *bonum coniugum* is clearly acknowledged as an essential aspect of marriage. Although the teaching makes

---

[40] See BURKE, "Progressive Jurisprudential Thinking," pp. 443-444.

[41] "A loro volta, entrambi i Codici da me promulgati, formulando la definizione del matrimonio, affermano che il 'consortium totius vitae' è 'per sua indole naturale ordinato al bene dei coniugi e alla generazione ed educazione dei figli' (CIC, can. 1055, §1; CCEO, can. 776, §1)" (JOHN PAUL II, Allocution to the Roman Rota, 1 February 2001, p. 7).

[42] "L'ordinazione alle finalità naturali del matrimonio – il bene dei coniugi e la procreazione ed educazione della prole – è intrinsecamente presente nella mascolinità e nell' femminilità. Quest'indole teleologica è decisiva per comprendere la dimensione naturale dell'unione. In questo senso, l'indole naturale del matrimonio si comprende meglio quando non la si separa dalla famiglia. Matrimonio e familia sono inseparabili, perché la mascolinità e la femminilità delle persone sposate sono costitutivamente aperte al dono dei figli. Senza tale apertura nemmeno ci potrebbe essere un bene dei coniugi degno di tal nome" (ibid.).

no reference to the juridical significance of the underlying concept, the explicit recognition of its place within the context of married life is, nevertheless, consistent in conciliar and magisterial teaching. In other words, the *good of the spouses*, whether understood as a good, an end or an element, holds a unique place in married life of the spouses and within the structure of marriage.

3. CONJUGAL LOVE AND *BONUM CONIUGUM*

The pastoral constitution, *Gaudium et spes*, attributed to genuine conjugal love a very special value that is fully human, personal and total. We read the following in GS 49: "That *love*, however, being eminently *human*, because it is directed from one person to another by affection of the will, embraces the good of the *whole person*. Therefore, it can enrich the expressions of the body and the spirit with a unique dignity and can ennoble them as the special elements and signs of the conjugal friendship. [...] Such a love, bringing together the human and divine, leads the spouses to a free and mutual giving of self, with tenderness demonstrated by action, and permeates their *whole lives* [...]"[43] According to this teaching, therefore, true and genuine conjugal love is an expression of and the dynamic force underlying the mutual total self-gift of the spouses. It pervades the whole of life of the spouses, and is not one-sidedly restricted to conjugal acts. The conjugal acts are, indeed, the culminating expression of that love and of its continual growth[44]. The council taught that marriage and conjugal love are essentially and intrinsically ordered to the raising up of new life[45]. Because of its all-pervading influence in married life, the council described marriage itself as an "intimate

---

[43] *GS* 49: "Ille autem *amor*, utpote eminenter *humanus*, cum a persona in personam voluntatis affectu dirigatur, *totius personae* bonum complectitur. Ideoque corporis animique expressiones peculiari dignitate ditare easque tamquam elementa ac signa specialia coniugalis amicitiae nobilitare valet. [...] Talis amor, humana simul et divina consocians, coniuges ad liberum et mutuum sui ipsius donum, tenero affectu ut opere probatum, conducit totamque vitam eorum pervadit;[...]" (*AAS*, 58 [1966], p. 1069; emphasis added).

[44] Ibid., p. 1070.

[45] *GS* 48: "Indole autem sua naturali, ipsum institutum matrimonii amorque coniugalis ad procreationem et educationem prolis orinantur iisque veluti suo fatigio coronantur." Also in *GS* 50, this teaching is repeated: "Matrimonium et amor coniugalis indole sua ad prolem procreandam et educandam ordinantur. Filii sane sunt praestantissimum matrimonii donum et ad ipsorum parentum bonum maxime conferunt" (ibid., p. 1067).

community of life" and "conjugal love" as its specifying element (no. 48)[46].

The Church's emphasis on the importance of conjugal love in married life has always been constant and unwavering. In his encyclical letter, *Arcanum divinae sapientiae*, of 10 February 1880, Leo XIII placed conjugal love among the categories of rights and obligations of marriage[47]. Pius XI, in his encyclical letter *Casti connubii*, gave primacy to love in marriage – not juridically as an end of marriage, but a primacy of honour. The goal of conjugal love and action flowing from it is to bring spouses toward the fulfilment of the potential in them that is interior and most characteristically human[48]. Pius XI, however, carefully avoided granting to conjugal love the status of the primary end or essence of marriage[49]. Similarly Pius XII, in his allocution of 29 October 1951 to the Italian Catholic Union of Midwives, acknowledged conjugal love as one of the essential *secondary ends* of marriage[50].

Paul VI, in *Humanae vitae*, described conjugal love as *fully human, total and exclusive,* and *fecund.* First he explained that marriage as a "wise and provident institution of God," is a sacrament representing "the union of Christ with his Church." Then he went on to identify "the characteristic features and exigencies of married love." "This love," he said, "is above all fully *human*, a compound of sense and spirit. [...] It is a love which is total – that very special form of personal friendship in which husband and wife generously share everything. [...] Again, married love is *faithful* and *exclusive* of all other, and this until death"[51]. The centrality of conjugal love in married life was emphasised in this magisterial teaching.

In *Familiaris consortio*, John Paul II spoke of marriage and family forming a communion of persons, serving life, participation in the formation of society and sharing in the life of the Church. He expressed the role of conjugal love in marriage as follows:

---

[46] Ibid.

[47] "Secundo loco sua utrique coniugum sunt officia definita, sua iura integre descripta. Eos scilicet ipsos necesse est sic esse animo semper affectos, ut *amorem maximum*, constantem fidem, sollers assiduumque praesidium alteri alterum debere intelligat" (LEO XIII, Encyclical letter *Arcanum divinae sapientiae*, 10 February 1880, in *Acta Sanctae Sedis*, 12 [1879-1880], pp, 385-402, here at p. 395).

[48] See *Casti connubii*, pp. 548-549.

[49] See Theodore MACKIN, *Marriage in the Catholic Church. What Is Marriage?*, New York/Ramsey, Paulist Press, 1982, p. 218.

[50] See *AAS*, 43 (1951), pp. 835-854.

[51] FLANNERY II, pp. 400-401.

> [...] conjugal love involves a totality, in which all the elements of the person enter – appeal of the body and instinct, power of feeling and affectivity, aspiration of the spirit and of will. It aims at a deeply personal unity, the unity that, beyond union in one flesh, leads to forming one heart and soul; it demands indissolubility and faithfulness in definitive mutual giving; and it is open to fertility (cf. *Humanae vitae*, 9). In a word it is a question of the normal characteristics of all natural conjugal love, but with a new significance which not only purifies and strengthens them, but raises them to the extent of making them the expression of specifically Christian values[52].

In his Rotal allocution of 21 January 1999, John Paul II speaks eloquently on the theological and juridical aspects of conjugal love[53]. First he distinguishes *authentic concept of conjugal love* from merely affective love. He says that authentic conjugal love is not to be confused with "a vague feeling or even a strong psycho-physical attraction [...] for another person, which consists of a sincere desire for his or her welfare and is expressed in a concrete commitment to achieve it. [...] A mere feeling is tied to the inconstancy of the human heart; mutual attraction alone, often stemming primarily from irrational and sometimes abnormal impulses, cannot have stability and is thus easily, if not inevitably, prone to fade"[54]. Therefore, *authentic amor coniugalis*

> is not only and not primarily a feeling, but is essentially a commitment to the other person, a commitment made by a precise act of will. It is this commitment which gives *amor* the quality of *coniugalis*. Once a commitment has been made and accepted through consent, love *becomes* conjugal and never loses this character. Here the fidelity of love, which is rooted in the freely assumed obligation, comes into play. In one of his meetings with the Rota my Predecessor, Pope Paul VI, said succinctly: "*From a spontaneous feeling of affection, love becomes a binding obligation (AAS, 68 [1976], 207)*"[55].

Thus, authentic conjugal love is rooted in the will of the parties. It consists in making a wilful choice of one's self-gift to the other and always seeks the good of the other. Thus the Holy Father finds an

---

[52] FLANNERY II, p. 825. This teaching has been repeated literally in the new *Catechism of the Catholic Church*, Revised Edition with amendments following the publication of the *Editio Typica* containing extended subject index and the Reader's Guide to Themes, Ottawa, Canadian Conference of Catholic Bishops, Concacan Inc., 1999, no. 1643, p. 368.

[53] JOHN PAUL II, Allocution to the Roman Rota, 21 January 1999, in *L'Osservatore romano*, Weekly English language edition, 10 February 1999, pp. 3 and 6.

[54] Ibid., p. 3.

[55] Ibid.

intrinsic link between conjugal love and the act of mutual consent, for
he says:

> But you jurists cannot overlook the principle that marriage consists essen-
> tially, necessarily and solely in the mutual consent expressed by those to be
> married. This consent is nothing other than the conscious, responsible
> assumption of a commitment through a juridical act by which, in reciprocal
> self-giving, the spouses promise total and definitive love to each other.
> They are free to celebrate marriage, after having chosen each other with
> equal freedom, but as soon as they perform this act they establish a per-
> sonal state in which love becomes something that is owed, entailing effects
> of a juridical nature as well[56].

It seems clear here that the Holy Father acknowledges the juridical
value of conjugal love. It is essentially an act of the will. In other words,
conjugal love enters, through the will of the spouses, into the juridic
order of marriage. It becomes the juridical object of conjugal consent
through which the spouses mutually give each other to constitute the
partnership of the whole of life. With this recognition of the juridical
nature of conjugal love, the Pope places its lack or absence within the
context of the defect of consent. Therefore, he says:

> In short, the simulation of consent, for example, means nothing other than
> giving the marriage rite a merely external value, without the corresponding
> will for a reciprocal gift of love, of exclusive love, of indissoluble love or
> of fruitful love. Is it any surprise that such a marriage is doomed to failure?
> Once the feeling or attraction dies, it lacks any element of internal cohe-
> sion. Missing is that reciprocal commitment of self-giving which alone can
> guarantee its permanence[57].

This clear theological-juridical approach to conjugal love adopted by
the Supreme Legislator of the Church is indeed unique. Even though he
does not explicitly state that conjugal love is an essential element of
marriage whose deliberate exclusion from consent could invalidate marriage under the provision of canon 1101, §2 (CCEO c. 824, §2), in my
opinion, he certainly seems to suggest such a possibility. In other words,
a deliberate will to exclude love in married life would amount to denial
of the legitimate right of one of the parties to an essential element of
marriage.

In the history of Rotal jurisprudence there has been only one sentence
which declared a marriage null on the basis of lack or absence of love

---

[56] Ibid.
[57] Ibid.

when consent was exchanged. In his affirmative decision of 30 October 1970, V. Fagiolo identified "conjugal love" with marital consent itself[58]. He specifically stated that where conjugal love is lacking either consent is not free, or it is not internal, or it excludes or limits the object which must remain integral in order to constitute a valid marriage. Conjugal love is identical to conjugal self-giving which is same as consent. In brief, conjugal love has a definite juridical significance not only in regard to the efficient cause of marriage but also in regard to the very essence of marriage.

In the case under consideration, the woman respondent had married the petitioner for two reasons: to run away from the rigid family environment and, hopefully, to get the life insurance of the petitioner in case he died during the war. She candidly admitted these reasons for marrying the petitioner. She truthfully confessed that she did not love the man at all. She had told her parents the day of the wedding that she would divorce the man if the marriage did not work out. That was exactly what happened. They separated within fifteen days after the wedding. Fagiolo interpreted this lack or absence of love on the respondent's part as identical to defect of consent. The respondent married solely for an extrinsic end which was contrary to the essence of Christian marriage. Therefore, Fagiolo argued that before the Second Vatican Council this was interpreted as simulation, but after the Council it must be considered as absence of consent due to defect of true conjugal love, because, in this case, there was no mutual marital self-gift by which marriage comes into being in the act of the celebration of marriage[59]. The Rotal *turnus* agreed that the woman excluded the indissolubility of marriage, but felt that the marriage was invalid due to a theologically and juridically much more serious reason, that is to say, for lack of authentic love on the woman's part.

---

[58] See decision *c*. FAGIOLO, 30 October 1970, in TRIBUNAL APOSTOLICUM SACRAE ROMANAE ROTAE, *Decisiones seu sententiae* (=RRT *Dec.*), 62 (1970), pp. 978-990. On page 982, Fagiolo states: "Videretur, ex iis quae diximus, amorem coniugalem esse matrimonii causam efficientem, sicut consensus. Imo, cum matrimonium sit proprie coniunctio maritalis, quae donationem mutuam postulat et intimam communitatem vitae gignit, videretur dici debere rectius amorem coniugalem cui proprium est donationem facere causam esse coniugii eumque matrimonium facere et esse."

[59] Ibid., p. 986: "At, dum in citata sententia et in quibusdam aliis [...] nullitas evincitur ex capite simulationis consensus tantum, nunc post Concilium videtur quod *defectum veri amoris coniugalis obiectum abest*, in casu, quia *deficit illa mutua donatio maritalis qua coniugium constituitur, in actu celebrationis matrimonii*." (emphasis added).

The theological and juridical reasons, derived directly from the conciliar teaching, on which Fagiolo supported the court's affirmative decision, reflect quite accurately the teaching of John Paul II discussed above. But the Holy Father explicitly speaks of simulation as the proper title for the invalidity arising from an absence or lack of "conjugal love" rather than to regard it as an autonomous ground, as Fagiolo had done.

The teaching of Pope John Paul II is clear as far as the relevance of conjugal love in marriage is concerned. It is an essential element of marriage. But the crucial question is whether love is so important to marriage that a marital union cannot come into existence without it. This question has practical relevance in certain cultures where the system of arranged marriages is a fact of life, and marital unions often begin without love but with a pledge, potential or aptitude for it. Can marriages contracted in such cultures be regarded as non-existent or non-sacramental merely because there was no love at the beginning? P. Palmer's reaction to Fagiolo's argument, in my opinion, is most appropriate to our study. For he says:

> My quarrel is only with the wording of the decision which speaks of the "lack of conjugal love" instead of the more precise "refusal to love." There have been and there will be many cultures in which engaged couples meet for the first time on the day of the marriage. This does not prevent them from pledging their love and undivided affection, even though love might be lacking at the time the covenant is entered[60].

In a similar vein, commenting specifically on the cultural variance in the relevance of "love" to marital consent, J. Prader says:

> The element of love does not have any essential juridic role in the constitutive act of marriage; if it had, then a large number of marriages would be invalid in those countries of Africa and of Near and Middle East, where even today frequently the spouses do not even have the possibility of knowing each other before marriage[61].

Prader, nevertheless, suggests that lack or absence of love can be an indication of the proof of simulation of consent. Or if such a lack of love is verified at the time of consent it could very well be a symptom of a serious psychological disorder capable of rendering the person afflicted by it incapable of assuming the essential obligations of marriage. But he

---

[60] See P.F. PALMER, "Needed: A Theology of Marriage," in *Communio*, 1 (1974), p. 248.
[61] Joseph PRADER, *Il matrimonio in Oriente e Occidente*, Kanonika 1, Roma, Pontificium Institutum Orientalium, 1992, p. 9.

insists, however, that merely lack of love in the beginning of marriage or its cessation during the marriage is *per se* not a motive for the invalidity of marriage[62].

The decision *coram* Fagiolo was appealed and judged subsequently *coram* Palazzini[63]. In his sentence, Palazzini admitted the integrative value of conjugal love in relation to *bonum fidei*, but denied it any essential juridical value. Palazzini's arguments were based on Navarrete's view according to which conjugal love is an "ajuridical" or "meta-juridical" element with no juridical importance. According to Navarrete, conjugal love is only an "integrative" and not a "constitutive" component of marriage[64].

In his address to the officials of the Rota, 9 February 1976, Paul VI made his personal intervention in this discussion and said that conjugal love is a force of the psychological order and, therefore, "conjugal love does not enter the purview of law"[65]. Consequently, he stated:

> We must, therefore, reject without qualification the idea that if a subjective element (conjugal love especially) is lacking in a marriage, the marriage ceases to exist as a juridical reality which originated in a consent once and for all efficacious. No, *the juridical reality continues to exist in complete independence of love:* it remains even though love may have totally disappeared[66].

The intervention of Paul VI on the matter at the time was timely as tribunals in several countries were trying to read into Fagiolo's sentence more than what he had tried to incorporate into his sentence on conjugal love. Paul VI was clear in stating that love is an element of the psychological order and not easily measurable according juridical criteria. Even though his allocution did not succeed in ending the discussion on the relevance of conjugal love to the validity of marriage, there has not been a single case judged at the Rota on the ground of lack or absence of true love in marriage since Fagiolo's sentence. But the interest in the matter has certainly not abated.

---

[62] Ibid.

[63] See decision c. PALAZZINI, 22 June 1971, in RRT *Dec.*, 63 (1971), pp. 467-479.

[64] See Urbano NAVARRETE, *Structura iuridica matrimonii secundum Concilium Vaticanum II: momentum iuridicum amoris coniugalis*, Roma, Pontificia Universitas Gregoriana, 1968, p. 154; IDEM, "Amor coniugalis et consensus matrimonialis," in *Quaedam problemata actualia de matrimonio*, tertia ed. notabiliter aucta, [ad usum privatum], Romae, Pontificia Universitas Gregoriana, 1979, p. 172.

[65] See *AAS*, 68 (1976), p. 207; English translation in *The Pope Speaks*, 21 (1976-1977), p. I53.

[66] Ibid.

Z. Grocholewski wrote in 1979 that the element of *amor benevolentiae* could assume essential juridical importance to the extent that it comes under the dominion of the will. In view of the nature of marriage as *communio vitae*, conjugal love is inseparably joined to marriage and should be accorded juridical importance in the same manner as the ordination of offspring and unity and indissolubility. Thus when this aspect of love (more accurately: the *right* to that essential nucleus of love) is excluded from matrimonial consent, the marriage itself should be declared null[67]. How can one determine the absence or substantial lack of this "essential nucleus of love" at the moment of exchanging consent?

Similarly G. Versaldi, after distinguishing rational, human love (equivalent to *amor benevolentiae*) from genital (erotic) and affective love, concludes that the former, insofar as it expresses the will to enter into the "communion of life" with another person, always has juridical importance, because it has an essential role to play in presenting the object of consent. Without this love, Versaldi says, there cannot be a valid marriage[68].

L. Wrenn, who prefers to define love as "an affective tendency toward another person which is dialogical in nature and which involves union with the other"[69], offers five reasons in favour of recognising the juridical significance of conjugal love in marriage. He argues that the "essence of the *bonum coniugum* consists in the *ius ad amorem*"[70]. Matrimonial consent is "essentially an act of love" through which the spouses "mutually *give and accept* each other" (canon 1057, §2) which, Wrenn maintains, is precisely what love is[71]. He explains the juridical relationship between conjugal love and *bonum coniugum* as follows:

> Our position does not claim that love is essential to marriage. Rather it claims first that *the right* to the *bonum coniugum* consists in part of the essential object of marital consent, and second, that the *bonum coniugum* consists not in partnership, companionship, caring, etc., but rather in the love of the parties for each other[72].

---

[67] See Zenon GROCHOLEWSKI, "De 'communione vitae' in novo schemate 'De matrimonio' et de momento iuridico amoris coniugalis," in *Periodica*, 68 (1979), p. 479.

[68] See G. VERSALDI, "Elementa psychologica matrimonialis consensus," in *Periodica*, 71 (1982), pp. 252-253; IDEM, "Via et ratio introducendi integram notionem christianam sexualitatis humanae in categorias canonicas," in *Periodica*, 75 (1986), pp. 412-413.

[69] See WRENN, "Refining the Essence of Marriage," p. 211.

[70] Ibid., p. 213.

[71] Ibid., p. 214.

[72] Ibid.

What is pledged at the time of consent is to love each other. Once this is done with sufficient understanding and willing, the marriage is valid and remains valid even if their love and commitment later disappears. Concluding his reflections on the juridic relevance of love and *bonum coniugum*, Wrenn says:

> If, therefore, the *ius ad amorem* came to be generally recognised in law as essential to marriage, then law and liturgy (not to mention sacramentology) would finally come together, and that, it seems to me, is right and just, *dignum*, and above all, *iustum*[73].

L. Chiappetta traces two tendencies prevalent in doctrine concerning this issue. He says that two distinct approaches can be identified in regard to the juridical relevance of conjugal love. First approach identifies conjugal love with matrimonial consent and, therefore, considers it as an essential element of marriage. Should one of the spouses exclude or be incapable of it, the marriage would be invalid. The second approach regards conjugal love in its psychological and ethical aspects as important or fundamental to marriage, but it has no juridical value. Because love pertains to the psychological sphere, it is no longer under the control of the will, rather it is a *metajuridical element*. Its absence does not constitute the invalidity of consent, but it can be an indication of invalidity or insufficiency of the matrimonial consent[74].

Chiappetta certainly acknowledges the importance of the above mentioned papal allocution, but he says that, as several authors maintain, in the teaching of Paul VI, conjugal love is seen as necessary for the realisation of the ends of marriage, but it is not an element juridically essential for the validity of marriage. Lack of love in marriage does not cause its nullity. It can certainly be an indication of lack of freedom, force and fear, simulation, etc. Nevertheless, Chiappetta argues that the pope's teaching seems clear as far as the affective and psychological aspects of love are concerned, but not in insofar as its *objective* and *deontological content*, that is to say, *love as an obligation intrinsic to communion of life*, is concerned. Such love constitutes an essential element of the matrimonial consent, and in this aspect its absence could constitute the nullity of marriage under canon 1101, §2 (CCEO c. 824, §2). In support of his reasoning, Chiappetta introduces the statement of John Paul II, which has reference precisely to this point. In his Rotal allocution of 28

---

[73] Ibid., p. 217.

[74] L. CHIAPPETTA, *Il matrimonio nella nuova legislazione canonica e concordatoria, manuale giuridico-patorale*, Roma, Edizioni Dehoniane, 1990, pp. 34-35, 238-239.

February 1982, the pope said: "The Council saw marriage as a covenant of love (see *GS*, no. 48) ... Speaking here of love, we cannot reduce it to love involving only the senses, to a passing attraction, to erotic sensation, to sexual impulse, to sentimental love, to the simple joy of living. Love is essentially a gift. Speaking of the act of love the Council envisages an act of giving, which is one, decisive, irrevocable because it is a total giving which wants to be and to remain mutual and fruitful"[75].

Chiappetta also draws arguments in favour of his view in a unique decision of the Apostolic Signatura dealing with a case from Utrecht (Holland)[76]. In this decision, which was pronounced through a special pontifical commission by a five judge (Cardinals) panel, the Signatura argued that love, accepted as an *erotic inclination*, cannot be accorded any juridical relevance, while, love understood as an *act of the will* manifested in accord with the norm of law is equivalent to *consent*. As an act of the will it cannot be confused with the inclination, passion, impulse or motive which leads the subject to eliciting it, and which can be different from affection and habit. The Signatura affirmed that love pertains to the efficient, intrinsic and essential cause of the marriage contract, and matrimonial consent could also be called the act of love[77].

According to Chiappetta, therefore, conjugal love understood in its *objective* and *deontological* sense, that is, as an obligation inherent to communion of life, is an essential element of marriage. For this reason, it can be the object of matrimonial consent, and consequently, of simulation.

While restating the teaching of Paul VI on the juridical relevance of conjugal love presented in his Rotal allocution of 1976, F. Bersini says: "With matrimonial consent the spouses mutually give not any gift, but themselves; not for a short period of time, but for their entire life. This total self-giving is inconceivable if it is not given with love. Only love enables the two persons of different sex to say to each other: 'I will be yours and forever – I will be yours and forever'"[78]. Even though Bersini

---

[75] JOHN PAUL II, Allocution to the Roman Rota, 28 February 1982, in WOESTMAN, *Papal Allocutions to the Roman Rota 1939-1994*, p. 172.

[76] This sentence has been published in several journals. See X. OCHOA, *Leges Ecclesiae post Codicem iuris canonici editae*, vol. V, *Leges annis 1973-1978 editae*, Roma, Commentarium pro Religiosis, 1980, n. 4419, col. 7092-7093; *Apollinaris*, 49 (1976), pp. 31-48; *Periodica*, 66 (1977), pp. 297-325; English translation in *CLD*, 8, pp. 769-790.

[77] See *CLD*, 8, pp. 781-782.

[78] Francesco BERSINI, *Il diritto canonico matrimoniale: commento giuridico-teologico-pastorale*, 4ª ed., Leumann (Torino), Editrice Elle Di Ci, 1994, p. 18.

does not discuss the juridic relevance of conjugal love, it seems evident that his view accords it great importance within the context of matrimonial consent, which is an act love.

In his in-depth study, which has taken into consideration several theological, anthropological and canonical aspects of conjugal love, M.F. Pompedda states: "This element is – as everybody knows – central and essential to marriage insofar as it is regarded above all in its initial and formative importance, as to be the *efficient cause* which cannot be substituted and suppressed by anyone"[79]. In concluding this excellent analysis, Pompedda identifies conjugal love with consent by saying: "ecco l'*atto di amore coniugale*, ecco insieme l'espressione dell'*authentico consenso matrimoniale*." Then he goes on to draw the two following conclusions which certainly seem to support the juridical relevance of conjugal love. He concludes:

> One who is not able to live out an *authentic conjugal love* is for that very reason incapable of assuming the essential obligations of marriage: I say *the essential* and not merely this or that obligation, by summing up in conjugal love, as we have described and understood, the essential nucleus of the marriage itself. Therefore, in the first place, the heterosexuality; then: a well-ordered sexuality (and this in a *human manner*), the fidelity, the totality of the obligation in terms of time, the good of the other as spouse, the openness to co-operation in creation, the openness to the education of children.
>
> In like manner, however, one who intentionally (with a positive act of the will or with error determining the same will: cc. 1099 and 1101), limits the dignified and at the same time the most human (more appropriately pertaining to "divine and human law") objective nucleus which is the essence of marriage, ends up rejecting, in fact rejects principally the *very concept of authentic conjugal love*. And in this manner the consent itself is substantially vitiated and is rendered null and nullifying[80].

---

[79] See M.F. POMPEDDA, "L'amore coniugale e il consenso matrimoniale," in *Quaderni di Studio rotale*, 7 (1994), p. 29: "Elemento questo è – come ognuno ben sa – del tutto centrale ed essenziale nel matrimonio, in quanto riguardato soprattutto nel suo momento iniziale e formativo, cosi da essere *causa efficiente* insostituibile e da nessuno insopprimibile."

[80] Ibid.: "Colui il quale non è capace di vivere un *autentico amore coniugale* è per ciò stesso incapace di assumere gli essenziali obblighi matrimoniali: dico *gli essenziali*, e non soltanto questo o quell'obbligho, sommandosi nell'amore coniugale, come lo abbiamo descritto ed inteso, il nucleo essenziale dello stesso matrimonio. E quindi, in primo luogo, la eterosessualtià, ma poi: una sessualità ordinata (ecco l'*umano modo*), la fedeltà, la totalità dell'impegno nel tempo, il bene dell'altro come coniuge, l'apertura all cooperazione creativa, la disponibilità alla educazione della prole.

Ma parimenti colui che intenzionalmente (con atto positivo di volontà o con errore specificante la volontà stessa: canoni 1099 e 1101) coarta quell'esaltante ed insieme

In light of the conciliar and papal teaching on marriage, conjugal love seems to acquire juridical relevance within the context of *bonum coniugum*. From the perspective of law, therefore, it is not any love, but the love which is specifically ordered to the good of spouses and of offspring as an expression of the "consortium totius vitae" is considered. This gives conjugal love an institutional or juridical character taking it out of the sphere of merely erotic or affective attraction and giving it stability as an element of *bonum coniugum*. If we consider conjugal love as an element of *bonum coniugum*, we must also admit that the meaning and, consequently, its elements may vary from one culture or society to another.

Rotal judges frequently include in their sentences excellent exposés on *conjugal love* while explaining the nature of marriage, but they deliberately refrain from discussing its juridical value for the concrete cases they deal with. For example, in his sentence of 16 December 1982, which was actually written after the 1983 Code was promulgated, in a case involving the disorder of anorexia nervosa, Stankiewicz presents the essential obligations of marriage within the context of *conjugal love* under two aspects highlighted by Pope John Paul II in his apostolic exhortation *Familiaris consortio*, n. 11:

> *a) Obligation to the gift of conjugal love, destined for the procreation and education of offspring, to be shared with the spouse perpetually and exclusively in a human way*[81].

It is not difficult to see in this statement the importance attributed to conjugal love. Conjugal love is considered here as a gift which leads the spouses to reciprocal "knowledge" of each other which makes them "one flesh." This *love* "does not end with the couple, because it makes them capable of the greatest possible gift, the gift by which they become co-operators with God for giving life to a new human person (*Familiaris consortio*, n. 14). In this relationship, *sexuality is realised in a truly human way if it is an integral part of the love by which a man and a woman mutually commit themselves totally to one another until death*" *(ibid., n. 11)*[82].

---

umanissimo (più esattamente attinente all 'divinum et humanum ius') nucleo oggettuale che è l'essenza del matrimonio, finisce per respingere, anzi principalmente respinge il *concetto stesso di autentico amore coniugale*. Ed in tal modo il consenso viene viziato sostanzialmente per divenire di fatto nullo e nullificante."

[81] C. STANKIEWICZ, 16 December 1982, in *EIC*, 39 (1983), p. 258.
[82] Ibid.

*b) Obligation to establish and preserve conjugal communion charac-
terised by unity and indissolubility (ibid., n. 20)*[83].

In these two statements, Stankiewicz identifies within the context of
"conjugal love" the essential rights and obligations which constitute the
consortium totius vitae. First, there is the "obligation" to conjugal love;
second, the "obligation" to orient this conjugal love to the "procreation" and "education" of offspring [with no mention of it's orientation
to *bonum coniugum*]; third, the "obligation" to share with the partner
this conjugal love a) "perpetually," b) "exclusively," and c) "in a
human way"; fourth, the "obligation" to *establish and preserve* "conjugal communion," which "demands total fidelity and indissoluble unity."

Stankiewicz's reflections seem to regard "conjugal love" as the
intrinsic force which enables spouses to realise the essential aspects of
their convenantal relationship. And yet, Stankiewicz does not call
"conjugal love" an essential element of marriage! In a more recent
article, he reiterates his position as follows: "Therefore, although the
very validity of the matrimonial bond is not subject to the element of
love[84], nevertheless conjugal love cannot be overlooked while assessing
either the conjugal duties, having taken into consideration that 'sexuality
is realised in a truly human way only if it is an integral part of the love
by which a man and woman commit themselves totally to one another
until death' [*FC* 11], or the conjugal communion itself, which is properly speaking the communion of conjugal love"[85]. This is the extent of
Stankiewicz's explanation of his position in regard to the juridical relevance of conjugal love to marriage consent.

An approach similar to that of Stankiewicz is evident also in the statements of other Rotal Auditors. For example, in his sentence of 19 July
1991, Bruno says: "However, true conjugal love is that which is not
merely erotic and sexual, but total with a perpetual gifting of one's soul
and body in responsible fecundity in accord with the laws established by
the Creator; this love fosters mutual help in good times and in bad, spiritual, religious and moral growth, as well as harmony in vigilant care
and upbringing of children, family peace, good social relationships,

---

[83] Ibid.

[84] Here Stankiewicz refers to two sentences in support of this conclusion: *c.* PINTO, 12
February 1982, in APOSTOLICUM ROTAE ROMANAE TRIBUNAL, *Decisiones seu sententiae*
(=RRT *Dec.*), 74 (1982), p. 65; *c.* EGAN, 22 April 1982, in ibid., pp. 202-215.

[85] Antoni STANKIEWICZ, "De iurisprudentia rotali recentiore circa simulationem
totalem et partialem (cc. 1101, §2 CIC; 824, §2 CCEO)," in *ME*, 122 (1997), p. 218.

etc."[86]. There is in this statement a clear affirmation of the relationship between conjugal love and *bonum coniugum*. However, while describing the function of conjugal love, Bruno does not speak a word about its juridical value. As a force intrinsic to the conjugal partnership it pervades all the essential aspects of the partnership, but *per se* it does not seem to assume any autonomous *caput*.

In brief, from a theological perspective, conjugal love, that is, the authentic love between two sexually distinct persons, ordered specifically to the *good of the spouses* and of offspring, is of the essence of marriage. It constitutes the inner dynamism which is indispensable to the survival of every conjugal union. This has been clearly affirmed by magisterial pronouncements and conciliar teaching on marriage. In juridical language we can express the same theological principle as follows: *the right to that conjugal love* which is ordered to the *good of the spouses* and of offspring is an essential element of marriage. Love itself does not have to be present at the time when two persons exchange their consent, as happens in many cultures even today. But this love must be pledged and the right exchanged either explicitly or implicitly in the act of consent. In other words, even in cultures where marriage may not begin with love, the right to authentic conjugal love must be exchanged in the act of consent. This implies that at the time of expressing consent both parties must be capable of loving and have the intention to love. If this essential right is substantially restricted in a marital consent, either because of a serious psychological disorder, which could render the person afflicted by it incapable of authentic conjugal love in married life, or because of an intention to reject it, the marriage can be declared invalid either in accord with canon 1095, 2° and/or 3° (CCEO c. 818, 2°-3°), or under partial simulation of canon 1101, §2 (CCEO c. 824, §2), because "conjugal love" is an essential element of marriage. If conjugal love assumes such an importance in the juridical order, what would be the canonical meaning and implications of *bonum coniugum* which is intrinsically linked to it?

4. CANONICAL MEANING OF *BONUM CONIUGUM*

The Code Commissions entrusted with the revision of ecclesiastical legislation for both the Latin and the Eastern Churches drafted canons on

---

[86] See decision *c.* BRUNO, 19 July 1991, in RRT *Dec.*, 83 (1991), p. 466.

marriage according to the wishes of the Council. The deliberations on the nature of marriage produced an oblique definition of marriage which reflects the substance of its description provided in *Gaudium et spes*, nn. 48-52. While still recognising the traditional institutional dimensions of marriage, the revised legislation defines it in personalistic terms as a covenant, by which a man and a woman establish between themselves a partnership of the whole of life, and which is ordered by its very nature to the *good of the spouses* and the procreation and education of offspring. It is of utmost importance to note what the legislator is doing here. He is saying that it is the "matrimonial covenant," the irrevocable personal consent of the parties, that is by its very nature ordered to the good of the spouses. In other words, the good of the spouses, together with the good of children, understood in its juridic sense, is necessarily included in the mutual consent (covenant) of the parties, because it is the first of the two natural ends of marriage.

The record of the deliberations of the *coetus* involved in revising marriage legislation, indicates that the insertion of the expression *bonum coniugum* into one of the earliest drafts of what was to become the present c. 1055, was approved unanimously and apparently without any difficulty[87]. The Code Commission deliberately rejected the request that the hierarchy of ends be restored in the new Code[88]; moreover, it also dismissed the objections against the introduction of *bonum coniugum* in canon 1055, §1, saying that its basis is found in the conciliar teaching on marriage as a covenant, a term rich in interpersonal meaning. Cardinal P. Felici's response:

> The expression "for the good of spouses" must remain. The ordering of marriage to the good of spouses is indeed an essential element of the matrimonial covenant and not the subjective end of those marrying[89].

The mind of the Legislator is clearly evident in this statement concerning the place of *bonum coniugum* within the structure of marriage. He is unequivocally endorsing the juridical relevance of the "good of spouses" by declaring that the marital covenant is "by its very nature

---

[87] See Communicationes, 9 (1977), p. 123. Also see Patrick J. CONNOLLY, *The Nature of Marriage as Proposed in the Codex iuris canonici and in the Codes canonum Ecclesiarum orientalium*, JCD diss., Ottawa, Saint Paul University, 1995, pp. 143-144; BURKE, "Progressive Jurisprudential Thinking," p. 443.

[88] See *Communicationes*, 3 (1971), p. 70.

[89] "Locutio 'ad bonum coniugum' manere debet. Ordinatio enim matrimonii ad bonum coniugum est revera elementum essentiale foederis matrimonialis, minime vero finis subiectivus nupturientis" (*1981 Relatio*, p. 244; *communicationes*, 15 [1983], p. 221).

ordered to the good of spouses and the procreation and education of off-spring." In light of this juridic approach to *bonum coniugum*, Burke concludes: "What is clear beyond question is that the *bonum coniugum* is presented in both the new Code and the 1994 Catechism as one of the two institutional *ends* of marriage. Analysis of the *bonum coniugum* sets out therefore with no doubt about its juridic classification, placing it within the category of an *end*"[90]. How do canonical writers view this *bonum coniugum*? While all recognised authors seem to admit that the good of the spouses can no longer be relegated to the juridically irrel-evant status of a secondary end of marriage, there is no agreement con-cerning its nature and content[91].

Immediately after the promulgation of the new Latin Code, J.M. Pinto discussed the juridical value of *bonum coniugum* in following terms:

> It seems the *essential elements of marriage* mentioned in canon 1101 of the new Code are to be derived from canon 1055, §1.
> The mind of the Consultors in formulating this canon was "to determine in what does marriage consist"[92]. The good of offspring and the good of spouses have already been established by the very Creator of nature as *fines operis*. Even if the end of a created thing is outside its essence, the *ordination* of offspring is essential to marriage, and in this ordination the good of the spouses is also included in its substance.
> Consequently, according to the norm of the new Code the *essential obliga-tions of marriage* are those which concern the good of offspring, the good of spouses, the good of fidelity and the good of sacrament. The partnership of the whole of life is "by its very nature" ordered to the first two (c. 1055, §1); the last two are the "essential properties of marriage"(c. 1056)[93].

---

[90] *C.* BURKE, 26 March 1998, p. 241.

[91] Ladislas ÖRSY, *Marriage in Canon Law:Texts and Comments, Reflections and Questions*, Wilmington, Delaware, Michael Glazier, 1988, p. 53; Luigi DE LUCA, "The New Law on Marriage," in *The New Code of Canon Law*, Michel THÉRIAULT and Jean THORN (eds), Ottawa, Faculty of Canon Law, Saint Paul University, vol. II, p. 831; Enrica MONTAGNA, "Considerazioni in tema di *bonum coniugum* nel diritto matrimoniale canon-ico," in *Il diritto ecclesiastico (=DE)*, 104, 3 (1993), pp. 663-703; Joan CARRERAS, "Il '*bonum coniugum*': oggetto del consenso matrimoniale," in *Ius Ecclesiae*, 6 (1994), pp. 117-158; J. Anthony DEWHIRST, "*Consortium vitae, bonum coniugum,* and Their Relation to Simulation: A Continuing Challenge to Modern Jurisprudence," in The Jurist, 55 (1995), pp. 794-812; Edward G. PFNAUSCH, "The Good of the Spouses in Rotal Jurispru-dence: New Horizons?" in *The Jurist*, 56 (1996), pp. 527-556; several interesting articles on this theme are contained in *Il "bonum coniugum" nel matrimonio canonico*, Studi iuridici XL, Città del Vaticano, Libreria editrice Vaticana, 1996; Cormac BURKE, "Pro-gressive Jurisprudential Thinking," in *The Jurist*, 58 (1998), pp. 437-478.

[92] See *Communicationes*, 9 (1977), p. 123, e.

[93] Josephus M. PINTO GOMEZ, "Incapacitas assumendi matrimonii onera in novo CIC," in *Dilexit iustitiam*, Studia in honorem Aurelii Card. Sabattani, curantibus Z. GROCHO-LEWSKI et V. CARCEL ORTI, Città del Vaticano, Libreria editrice Vaticana, 1984, p. 23.

Pinto saw *bonum coniugum* as a natural end of marriage, and the *ordination* of the marriage covenant to this good must be included within the substance of marriage consent. Thus, Pinto clearly acknowledged the ordination of marriage to the good of the spouses as an essential element of marriage.

M.F. Pompedda, who has written extensively on the different aspects of marriage, also has showed no hesitation in admitting the juridical relevance of *bonum coniugum* within the canonical schema of marriage. He includes *bonum coniugum* in his essential definition of marriage which is a) a *consortium* between a *man* and a *woman*; b) a *consortium* of the whole of life; c) perpetual and exclusive; d) directed toward the good of the spouses, and e) toward the generation and raising of offspring[94].

In the final analysis, Pompedda explains that marriage receives its determination both from its direction toward the good of the spouses and from its direction toward the good of offspring, under the aspect of the intimate community or union of life[95]. However, he acknowledges the serious difficulty in fully grasping this reality. He says:

> What is meant by the term: the conjugal good (the *bonum*)? This must be left to jurisprudence and to your further study and reflection.[...] In Italian we would say that this word "conjugal" as it is used in CIC/1983 is *"pregnante"* or *"filled"* with meaning. It is a most profound expression. The CIC/1983 says *bonum coniugum* and it does not say *ad bonum alterius coniugis*. This means it is both the good of the person in himself/herself *and* the good of the other; but *both* to the extent that they are both co-participants in the same reality, the same *consortium* which is matrimony. Having said this however, we must be careful: we are in the context of what is essential. We must not confuse what is essential with what is non-essential in this *conjugal* good[96].

Pompedda's *caveat* highlights three important points. First, the phrase *bonum coniugum* is in fact "filled" with meaning and is certainly not as simple as some seem to consider it to be. Second, the phrase implies the good of both spouses and not just of one of the spouses. Third, even in this *bonum* there are elements which are essential and others which are non-essential. As understood in our context, the non-essential elements or qualities are of no juridical consequence. Our focus for the purpose of

---

[94] Mario F. POMPEDDA, "Incapacity to Assume the Essential Obligations of Marriage," in *Incapacity for Marriage: Jurisprudence and Interpretation*, Acts of the III Gregorian Colloquium, Robert M. SABLE (Coordinator and Editor), Rome, Pontificia Universitas Gregoriana, 1987, p. 192.

[95] Ibid., p. 188.

[96] Ibid., p. 192.

determining the essence of *bonum coniugum* must be on those elements which are considered essential.

An author who has contributed most to the debate on the juridical relevance of *bonum coniugum* is C. Burke. He continues to argue that *bonum coniugum* cannot be an essential element or property of marriage. This is what he says in his latest sentence cited above: "If it is an end it cannot be an essential property or element of marriage"[97]. "The properties necessarily enter the essence; so too does the ordination to the end. But the actual end itself remains extrinsic to the essence, for the end may fail ever to be achieved, without the essence failing in its existence"[98]. Finally:

> We repeat that all the logic of philosophical and juridic discourse, working from these fine but clear distinctions, makes it evident that since the *bonum coniugum* is an end of marriage, *it is not and cannot be* one of its essential elements or properties. Only if this is appreciated and accepted as a fundamental guiding principle for discussion, can one develop a coherent analysis of the *bonum coniugum*. Nevertheless, suggestions are still made to the effect not only that the *bonum coniugum* is an essential element of marriage *rather than an end* but, even more peculiarly, that is indifferently an essential element *and* an end at one and the same time. While these suggestions do not stand up to examination, they are to be found, and constitute a source of considerable confusion[99].

U. Navarrete puts forward a similar view on this matter. In his critical analysis of this issue, he seems hesitant to acknowledge "*bonum coniugum*" as an essential element of the object of consent. He argues that both doctrine and jurisprudence have always regarded it as an end of marriage, and ends are extrinsic to the essence. Nevertheless, he seems to admit that "*bonum coniugum*" can be considered a fourth "*bonum*" which may be regarded as an essential element of marriage according to c. 1101, §2. In the final analysis, however, he says that "the use of the term '*bonum coniugum*' in two fundamentally different contexts, that is to say, in that of ends and of essential elements of consent is not methodologically acceptable"[100].

---

[97] *C.* BURKE, 26 March 1998, p. 243; also see BURKE, "Progressive Jurisprudential Thinking," pp. 444-452.

[98] *C.* BURKE, 26 March 1998, p. 245.

[99] Ibid., p. 249.

[100] See Urbano NAVARRETE, "I beni del matrimonio: elementi e proprietà essenziali," in *La nuova legislazione matrimoniale canonica: il conenso: elementi essenziali, difetti, vizi*, Studi giuridici X, Città del Vaticano, Libreria editrice Vaticana, 1986, pp. 97-98. "Ora l'uso del termine 'bonum coniugum' in due contesti fondamentalmente diversi, vale a dire in quello dei fini e in quello degli elementi essenziali del consenso non é metodologicamente accettabile" (ibid., p. 98).

On the other hand, Pompedda presents a different argumentation in support of considering the end of marriage as its essential element. He maintains that in interpreting law we cannot proceed from scientific or doctrinal theories. "The person who applies law cannot take recourse to particular doctrines even though they may have some type of authority, as they are not clear determinations of law [...]. Scientific though such theories may be, one must remember always that these are nothing more than theories"[101]. The canonist, Pompedda continues, is interested in determining the essence of marriage within the context of the canons. The canonist must apply the Code. He/she cannot go outside the Code to theories no matter how authoritative or how most authoritative they may be. Such doctrinal theories cannot provide the objective security needed to interpret the Code[102].

What follows from the above argument of Pompedda is that the essence of marriage and its essential elements and properties are to be derived directly from the canons of the Code and not from theories. All the essential elements and properties are included either explicitly or implicitly in the relevant canons. The Legislator has determined the essential definition of marriage in canon 1055, §1 (CCEO c. 776, 1§), he has clearly stated in canon 1056 (CCEO c. 776, §3) what the essential properties of marriage are; he has indicated in canon 1101, §2 (CCEO c. 824, §2) that there are essential elements which constitute marriage, and these are to be derived from canon 1055, §1 (CCEO c. 776, §1). After formulating the essential definition of marriage from the relevant canons, Pompedda concludes that a threefold element, which constitutes the essence of matrimony can be differentiated. The first element: the *consortium* of the whole of life between the man and the woman. The second element: a twofold direction or finality, namely a consent directed toward the *bonum coniugum* and toward the *procreation and raising of offspring*[103]. In a recent article, Pompedda reiterates this same argument. In essence he says that it is the Legislator who determines what is the essence of marriage, its essential properties and essential elements. And Pompedda does not seem to have any hesitation in considering the natural ordinations of marriage as essential elements of marriage[104].

---

[101] POMPEDDA, "Incapacity to Assume the Essential Obligations," p. 181.
[102] Ibid.
[103] Ibid., p. 186.
[104] See Mario F. Pompedda, "Il canone 1095, nn. 2-3 nell'economia della disciplina canonica del matrimonio," in *L'incapacità di intendere e di volere nel diritto matrimoniale canonico*, Studi iuridici LII, Città del Vaticano, Libreria editrice Vaticana, 2000,

Wrenn says: "In light of the Second Vatican Council and of the 1983 Code, the answer is crystal clear. The answer is that besides the three *bona* recognised prior to Vatican II, we now know that there is a fourth *bonum* which is equally essential to marriage, namely the *bonum coniugum*"[105].

After a careful analysis of the debate over whether the *bonum coniugum* should be treated as a fourth *bonum* or be absorbed into the *tria bona* model, C. Scicluna concludes: "[...] canonical doctrine and jurisprudence should a) continue to adopt the *tria bona* model (without the unnecessary introduction of a fourth "*bonum coniugum*"), or b) adopt the four-fold model of the two essential properties and the two "*ordinationes*"[106]. It seems obvious from his discussion of the historical and canonical development of the *tria bona* model, Scicluna opts for the first proposal. For he says: "Of these two possibilities the first one, that of the continued adoption of the *tria bona* model, is to be preferred because it better ensures the necessary space for further development. The determination of the essential rights and obligations which are at the basis of the determination of the essential formal object of marriage consent and the capacity to assume the marriage commitment could also be developed on the lines and with the aid of the *tria bona* model"[107].

What is the content of *bonum coniugum*? This question continues to be debated. In current canonical literature there is often reference to the essential rights and duties constitutive of *bonum coniugum* under the headings of "*ius ad vitae communionem*," "*relatio interpersonalis*," "*mutuum adiutorium*," etc.[108]. Such an approach is certainly misleading and confusing to say the least. Scicluna correctly maintains that these

---

p. 24. Here he says: "Ma è certo che il Legislatore non ha avuto difficoltà a qualificare come *essenziali* tali proprietà; ed anche gli elementi sono stati qualificati con l'aggettivo *essenziali* e peraltro tali debbono essere riconosciute quelle due ordinazioni naturali del connubio.

"In realtà, il *fine*, in quanto è termine del dinamismo di un qualsiasi ente finito, è necessariamente esterno e quindi distinto dall'essenza. Ma tra l'essenza e il fine esiste una non meno *necessaria connessione*. L'essenza cioè, quando è rapportata al fine o ai fini per il quale o per i quali essa esiste, in se stessa deve contenere lo stesso o gli stessi fini."

[105] See WRENN, "Refining the Essence of Marriage," p. 204.

[106] Scicluna, *The Essential Definition of Marriage*, p. 304.

[107] Ibid.

[108] See, for example, Valeria LUCCHETTI, *Il bonum coniugum nel matrimonio canonico: contenuti e classificazione*, JCD diss., Pescara, [Pontificia Studiorum Universitas A. S. Thoma Aq. In Urbe, 1998, pp. 58-64, where several concepts related to *bonum coniugum* are presented by some local tribunals without serious discussion.

concepts either stand for the totality of *matrimonium in facto esse* or are ambiguous[109].

There are at least two schools of thought on the content of *bonum coniugum*[110]. According to the first school, the *bonum coniugum* and conjugal love are identical. This may be clearly seen in Wrenn's writings. He discusses six of the more obvious qualities that might constitute the essence of "*bonum coniugum*," namely *partnership, benevolence, companionship, friendship, caring,* and *love*. All these qualities coalesce into genuine love. Therefore, genuine love is the essence of *bonum coniugum* and the *ius ad amorem* should be recognised in law as essential to marriage[111]. The proponents of the second view consider *bonum coniugum* as distinct from conjugal love. This view is founded on the conciliar conception of the human person and it identifies the *bonum coniugum* with the will of each spouse to involve oneself in the psychological, physical, and spiritual well-being and perfection of the other within the context of married life[112]. For example, L. De Luca says that the "good of spouses" ought to be seen, above all, as the *spiritual good* of the spouses[113]. It is this latter view, in my opinion, that seems to offer a much wider foundation for jurisprudential determination of the content of *bonum coniugum* seen from a socio-cultural perspective.

It is important here to advert to the approach taken by Burke concerning the juridical value of *bonum coniugum*. As already mentioned above, he admits that "the orientation of marriage to the good of the spouses" is of the essence of marriage. He argues: "There can be no doubt that the exclusion of the *bonum coniugum* – the other end of marriage – similarly invalidates. However, once we raise the questions of what exactly is involved in practice in this latter exclusion, as well as how such cases are best handled in tribunal work, we once more find ourselves in an area of considerable opinion and debate"[114]. How would he handle such a case? His answer is: "So, while exclusion of *bonum coniugum* of course invalidates matrimonial consent, the opinion of the undersigned simply does not favour pressing it forward as grounds in a case which is

---

[109] See SCICLUNA, *The Essential Definition of Marriage*, p. 300.

[110] See L. ORTAGLIO, "Breve ricostruzione dello stato della dottrina e della giurisprudenza intorno al *bonum coniugum*," in *Ius et munera*, G. GIUSTINIANO, ed., Naples, Laurenziana, 1997, pp. 109-118, where these two schools of thought are further explained.

[111] See WRENN, "Refining the Essence of Marriage," p. 217.

[112] See ORTAGLIO, "Breve ricostruzione dello stato della dottrina e della giurisprudenza," p. 112.

[113] See DE LUCA, "The New Law on Marriage," p. 831.

[114] See *c.* BURKE, 26 March 1998, p. 269.

almost certainly going to be better handled under deceit, or under partial or total simulation in their traditional connotation"[115]. In other words, his preference is to absorb the exclusion of *bonum coniugum*, which is a legitimate ground of nullity of marital consent, into the traditional augustinian *bona*. Why? Because, *"bonum coniugum"* is not a property but an end, and it consists "in that maturing of the persons and characters of the spouses which comes from fidelity to the married commitment, from living marriage in accordance with its essential properties"[116]. In another article he repeats the argument that this *bonum* consists fundamentally in the maturing of the spouses for the ultimate purpose of life. It is precisely to this that marriage, when lived according to its essential properties, tends[117]. In another study published the same year, he concludes: "For our purpose, in any case, essential elements and essential rights and obligations are not the same thing; essential rights and obligations have to be derived from the essential elements. For instance, if one can say that the *ordination ad bonum coniugum* is an essential element, then the rights and obligations deriving from it coincide with those deriving from the three augustinian *bona*. It is these that provide the basis for defining the essential rights and obligations through the fulfilment of which marriage can attain its institutional ends"[118].

The direct consequence of this view for jurisprudence is obvious. As an end, this *bonum* falls outside the essence of marriage. Therefore, one cannot use the expression *"ius ad bonum coniugum."* Marriage can exist without the achievement of this *bonum*. While each party has the right that the other accept marriage in its essential integrity (with its essential properties), neither can claim the end(s) of marriage as a right. Therefore, one cannot correctly speak of a *right* to the *bonum coniugum*. What each spouse can claim, as a matter of right, is that the natural ordering of marriage to the good of the spouses be not excluded from one's consent[119]. According to Burke's view, cases where marriage is invalid

---

[115] Ibid., p. 271; also see BURKE, "Progressive Jurisprudential Thinking," p. 461.

[116] See Cormac BURKE, "The *Bonum coniugum* and the *bonum prolis*: Ends or Properties of Marriage?" in *The Jurist*, 49 (1989), p. 708.

[117] Cormac BURKE, "Some Reflections on Canon 1095," in *ME*, 117 (1992), p. 135.

[118] Cormac BURKE, "The Essential Obligations of Matrimony," in *Studia canonica*, 26 (1992), p. 398. A more extensive treatment of this theme may be found also in his: "Marriage: A Personalist or an Institutional Understanding?" in *Communio*, 19 (1992), pp. 278-303; Burke returns to this theme again in "Progressive Jurisprudential Thinking," pp. 450-452.

[119] BURKE "The *Bonum coniugum* and *bonum prolis*: Ends or Properties of Marriage?" p. 709.

due to the exclusion of the *bonum coniugum*, considered as an autonomous ground of nullity, may very well be rare from the nature of things[120]. His preference is, therefore, to consider the cases of alleged exclusion of the good of the spouses under the three traditional augustinian *bona*. In his recent article, Burke proposes that the augustinian *bona* can be most useful in incorporating into jurisprudence the personalism of marriage advocated by the council. He claims that the augustinian *tria* bona are essentially positive and personalist in nature. And a positive and personalist appreciation of these *bona* contribute to appropriate jurisprudential approach to the nature and content of marriage[121].

In my considered opinion, the approach adopted by the Second Vatican Council, by the Pontifical Commission for the Revision of the Code, and ultimately by the Legislator himself, is not the one circumscribed by the augustinian schema. The very nature of marriage necessitates an approach that would take into consideration the different cultural dimensions of marriage. The Council described marriage as a human reality, an exclusive and permanent *union* or *communio* of a man and a woman ordered toward the good of the spouses and generation and upbringing of children, and between two validly baptised persons it is graced with sacramental dignity. Through the application of valid canonical principles, as Pompedda argues, most canonical writers have concluded that the "*bonum coniugum*" is of the essence of marriage (whether one considers it an intrinsic end, an element or a property), each spouse has a right to that *bonum*. And its exclusion from consent either due to an *incapacity* or through a *positive act of the will* renders marriage invalid. Prevalent Rotal jurisprudence confirms this approach.

We know that a human person is a psychobiological and spiritual being not totally amenable to scientific studies. Any description of the

---

[120] See ibid., p. 708; also see his sentence of 26 March 1998, p. 271. Jurisprudence does not seem to support this view of Burke. For example, in several recent sentences we witness a definite tendency toward acknowledgement of the right to *bonum coniugum* as an essential element of marriage. For example, we read the following conclusion in a case involving schizophrenia: "[...] concludi debet morali cum certitudine mulierem conventam ad nuptias accessisse sub effectu eiusdem morbi, qui quamvis in stadio incubationis proxime erumpens esset, eiusdem perturbavit voluntatem et incapacem reddidit essentiales obligationes matrimonii, quae ad *bonum coniugum* et ad *procreationem et educationem prolis* natura sua ordinantur assumere, et effectum perducere" (c. PALESTRO, 6 June 1990, in *ME*, 116 [1991], p. 378; emphasis added). For a similar approach, also see c. BRUNO, 19 July 1991, in ROTAE ROMANAE TRIBUNAL, *Decisiones seu sententiae* (=RRT *Dec.*), 83 (1991), pp. 476-477.

[121] See BURKE, "Progressive Jurisprudential Thinking," pp. 466-471.

good of the spouses must take into account the totality of the human person and the duality of conjugal relationship. The term *bonum coniugum* is an all-embracing expression implying physical, emotional, intellectual, and spiritual well being of the couple[122].

Because matrimonial covenant involves the *whole* person of each spouse and of both spouses together, in determining the essence of *bonum coniugum* one must consider the physical, emotional, mental, sexual, moral-ethical, and spiritual well being of both spouses. Both Scripture and magisterial teaching focus on the *perfection* and *fulfilment* of the *whole person* of the spouses and of the *"two-in-one-flesh"* reality. In married state both spouses have the right/obligation to a *reasonable degree* of interior perfection of their being, the right/obligation to their physical integrity, to their individuality and personal dignity, to a life that will foster mutual growth towards the realisation of the meaning carved into their "two-in-one-flesh" existence. Therefore, Örsy correctly points out that "to enter marriage with the purpose of personal fulfilment only is to bring into it the seed of destruction; a person doing so would not be dedicated to the true value of the married state"[123].

As with the other essential elements of marriage, the essence of this *bonum* is to be determined gradually through developing jurisprudence which should naturally take into consideration its cultural contexts, because "conjugal good" is not something abstract but concrete, situated in the existential dimension of the spouses[124]. Moreover, it is also important to distinguish between those elements that are not of the essence of this good, and those which are of its essence. Doctrine and jurisprudence have consistently drawn our attention to this point. It is the task of canonical doctrine and jurisprudence to identify the essential elements that constitute the *bonum coniugum*.

5. JURISPRUDENTIAL APPROACHES TO *BONUM CONIUGUM*

There is now universal acceptance of the ordination of the covenant of marriage (cf. *GS* 48 and c. 1055, §1; CCEO c. 776, §1) or of the *consortium totius vitae* (cf. Rotal allocution of 2001) to *bonum coniugum* as an essential element of marriage. However, the exact nature of this

---

[122] See ÖRSY, Marriage in Canon Law, p. 53.
[123] Ibid.
[124] See WRENN, Refining the Essence of Marriage," pp. 205-206.

bonum is still being debated, at times with great interest and intensity, in canonical circles. But the fact that the ordination of marriage to *bonum coniugum* can be the object either of incapacity of c. 1095 (CCEO c. 818) or of exclusion(s) mentioned in c. 1101, §2 (CCEO c. 824, §2) is peacefully admitted in canonical doctrine and jurisprudence. Even Burke, who does not seem to shy away from discouraging the use of *bonum coniugum* as a source of autonomous grounds of nullity, writes: "So while I naturally hold that exclusion of *bonum coniugum* invalidates matrimonial consent, I am not in favour of forcing it forward as grounds in a case which is almost certainly going to be better handled under *dolus*, or under partial or total simulation in their traditional connotation"[125]. A similar view is being expressed by him also in regard to the ground of incapacity. He says that "we are certainly walking in too dim a light to be able to speak with any assurance about what a capacity or incapacity for the 'good of the spouses' actually involves." Then he adds, "We return to the same observation: far more precise study of the nature of the *bonum coniugum* is needed before we can speak, with juridic precision, about the essential obligations of marriage"[126]. At least the experience of the Rotal court in handling cases of exclusion of the good of the spouses seems to confirm Burke's concern because he himself states: "As far as my research has ascertained, not a single Rotal case since the 1983 code has been judged on the grounds of the exclusion of the *bonum coniugum*"[127]. While this is true as far as Rotal jurisprudence is concerned, local tribunals have not shown such hesitation in considering the juridic relevance of *bonum coniugum* in concrete cases[128]. This is not the situation at the Rota, however, with regard to the incapacity cases. For the purpose of this study I will present a brief analysis of a few selected recent Rotal sentences which have dealt with this *bonum* insofar as they refer to incapacity mentioned in c. 1095 (CCEO c. 818).

On 30 May 1986 a marriage case from Hexam and New Castle (Great Britain) was judged *coram* Pinto[129]. The woman petitioner in the case

---

[125] BURKE, "Progressive Jurisprudential Thinking," p. 461.

[126] Ibid., p. 463.

[127] Ibid., p. 460; Burke repeats the same in his above cited sentence of 26 March 1998, p. 271.

[128] See LUCCHETTI, *Il bonum coniugum nel matrimonio canonico*, pp. 59-64, where a brief discussion of some Italian cases involving exclusion of *bonum coniugum* is presented.

[129] See decision *c*. PINTO, 30 May 1986, in *ME*, 111 (1986), pp. 389-395. English translation in *Matrimonial Decisions of Great Britain and Ireland for 1989*, vol. 25, pp. 46-49. This sentence remains unpublished in the 1986 volume of *Decisiones*. See RRT *Dec.*, 78 (1986), p. XVI, #87.

alleged that her husband was suffering from grave *lack of discretion of judgement* and *incapacity to assume and to fulfil the essential obligations of marriage* at the time of exchanging consent. The decision of the first instance court was negative on both grounds. The appeal tribunal ruled affirmatively only on the ground of *incapacity to assume and fulfil the essential obligations of marriage,* and negatively on lack of discretion of judgement. Thus there remained only the ground of "incapacity to assume" to be responded to by the Rotal court.

Because the marriage relationship in the case suffered serious problems due to physical and emotional violence toward the wife caused by alcohol abuse and gambling related problems of the husband, and because the second instance court had explicitly referred to the respondent's incapacity to provide for the good of the spouse in marriage, Pinto makes a brief statement in regard to *bonum coniugum.*

Pinto says that the *good of spouses* includes those obligations without which it would be at least morally impossible to have that intimate joining of persons and activities by which the spouses mutually provide help and service to each other, and to which marriage is by its nature ordered as well (*GS* 48). Where this integration of persons and of activities is gravely deficient, communion of life, that is, the partnership of conjugal life in which marriage essentially consists becomes impossible (c. 1055, §1)[130]. This is the concept of *bonum coniugum* which Pinto has consistently proposed in his sentences and writings[131]. He does not, however, explain or identify the exact nature or content of *bonum coniugum.*

Pinto admits that the disorder of alcoholism could be a legitimate cause of incapacity to assume the essential obligations of marriage. He also acknowledges that pathological gambling can similarly invalidate consent under the same conditions. In other words, both these disorders either individually or in combination can render a person incapable of assuming the essential obligations flowing from *bonum coniugum*[132].

The evidence in this case clearly attested to serious psychological problems in the respondent. His developmental background within the

---

[130] "*Bonum coniugum* complectitur obligationes illas sine quibus est saltem moraliter impossibilis intima personarum atque operum coniunctio, qua coniuges adiutorium et servitium mutuo sibi praestant, et ad quam coniugum ex natura sua ordinatur etiam [...]. Haec personarum operumque integratione graviter deficiente, impossibilis fit vitae communio seu consortium vitae coniugalis in quo matrimonium essentialiter consistit (cfr. can. 1055, §1)" (*ME,* 111 [1986], p. 390).

[131] See PINTO GOMEZ, "Incapacitas assumendi matrimonii onera," pp. 29,36, 37; decision *c.* PINTO, 9 November 1984, in *ME,* 110 (1985), p. 321.

[132] See *ME,* 111 (1986), p. 390.

immediate family context suggested the possibility of negative familial influences on his personality. He himself admitted his problems with alcohol, gambling and infidelity. There was also indisputable evidence of violence toward his spouse and gross neglect of the spouse and children. The most crucial question that needed to be answered in this case was whether the alleged pathological mental state (alcoholism, pathological gambling, persistent infidelity, etc.) of the respondent was really present, at least **latently**, at the time of exchanging matrimonial consent. While Pinto's *turnus* admitted the existence of serious problems in married life, it regarded them only as post-nuptial in origin, that is, the result of a stressful marital situation. The decision of the *turnus* was: "Therefore, there is no proof of incapacity on respondent's part *to assume the obligation of the good of the spouses in relation to his wife*"[133].

This sentence explicitly deals with the incapacity to assume the obligation of *bonum coniugum*. Although the decision is negative, Pinto reaffirms the juridic relevance of the concept of *bonum coniugum* promoted by the council. His sentence demonstrates that the ground of incapacity to assume the obligation of *bonum coniugum* is legally sustainable and applicable to concrete cases in accord with the norms of law.

On 11 July 1991, a case from Dallas, Texas, was judged coram Bruno[134] on grounds of "lack of due discretion" or "incapacity to assume the obligations on the part of both"[135]. The first instance decision was affirmative presumably on both grounds on the part of both parties. The respondent appealed directly to the Rota, where Bruno, the *ponens*, determined the doubt as follows: "*Whether there is proof of invalidity of marriage in the case due to incapacity to assume conjugal obligations according to the mind of c. 1095, 3° on the part of both parties*"[136].

---

[133] "Non ergo constat de incapacitate conventi assumendi onus boni coniugum relate ad uxorem. Quodsi testis C. affirmat: 'Non posso proprio immaginarlo che si potesse adattare con alcuna. Sono sicuro che egli sarà sempre stesso' [...], nempe absolute incapax ad nuptias contrahendas, de hoc infra sermo erit cum de sanatione syndromum agemus" (ibid., p. 394).

[134] See decision *c.* BRUNO, 11 July 1991, in RRT *Dec.*, 83 (1991), pp. 461-477.

[135] Ibid., p. 464: "Se la nullità del matrimonio è stata provata per la causale di vizio del consenso per mancanza della dovuta discrezione o incapacità di assumere gli obblighi da entrambe le parti."

[136] Ibid.: "An constet de matrimonii nullitate, in casu, ob partium incapacitatem assumendi onera coniugalia ad mentem can. 1095, n. 3."

In his reflections on the provision of canon 1055, §1 in light of conciliar teaching on marriage, F. Bruno argues:

> The 1917 Code made a distinction between the primary ends of marriage (the procreation and education of offspring) and the secondary ends (mutual help and remedy of concupiscence) (cf. c. 1013, §1). The new Code, on the other hand, has suppressed the distinction between the primary and secondary ends of marriage, and by proposing *bonum coniugum* and making it equal to *procreation and education of offspring*, all the primary and secondary ends are unified in them[137].

According to Bruno, the substance of the norm acknowledges, besides the procreation of offspring, also the achievement of *personal fulfilment* of the spouses through their self-giving as an essential element of marriage. He says:

> The good of the spouses as an end and as an essential element of the nuptial covenant, is the sum total of all goods which flow from the interpersonal relationships of the same spouses. If they do not suffer from any psychic anomaly of personality, they together, through appropriate interpersonal relationships, enrich each other as individual persons and the entire conjugal life[138].

Although Bruno's use of terms in this statement seem juridically imprecise and could in fact be misleading if not understood properly, what is important to note is his acknowledgement of the "enrichment of individual persons and the entire conjugal life" (this is exactly the core of the *bonum coniugum*) as an essential element of marriage.

The testimonial evidence and two expert opinions obtained by the courts in this case confirmed that the respondent was suffering from a serious mental disorder known in psychiatry as passive-aggressive personality disorder. On the basis of this clinical information, Bruno's *turnus* stated: "And in this way he was incapable of establishing not

---

[137] "Codex Piano-Benedictinus anni 1917 distinctionem faciebat inter matrimonii fines primarios (procreationem ed educationem prolis) et fines secundarios (mutuum adiutorium et sedationem concupiscentiae) (cf. can. 1013, §1). Novus Codex, e contra, distinctionem supprimit, et bonum coniugum primo proponens illudque *aequans* cum *procreatione et educatione prolis*, videtur in iisdem omnes fines primarios et secundarios unificare" (c. BRUNO, 19 July 1991, pp. 465-466; emphasis added).

[138] *C.* BRUNO, 19 July 1991, p. 466: "Bonum coniugum, uti finis et elementum essentiale nuptialis foederis, est veluti omnium bonorum summa, quae promanant ex relationibus interpersonalibus eorumdem coniugum. Ipsi enim, si nulla personalitatis psychica anomalia laborent, per adaequatas relationes interpersonales, insimul seipsos ditant, uti singulas personas, et totam vitam coniugalem."

only the *consortium totius vitae* but also a deep friendly relationship"[139]. In concluding his decision, Bruno states:

> Hence, after carefully considering the gravity and antecedence of the cause of a psychic nature [passive-aggressive personality disorder], which had become serious, we must conclude, supported also by the opinion of experts as having foundation in the acts, that the respondent was incapable of assuming the essential obligations of marriage, particularly those *which form the foundation of the good of the spouses, the constitutive element of marriage*, toward which the conjugal covenant of its very nature is ordered[140].

One important point seems to stand out in this sentence of Bruno, that is to say, the ordination of the marital *consortium* to the good of the spouses is intrinsic to marriage and its exclusion due to a serious psychological disorder could invalidate consent. What is not clear in this sentence, however, is the exact nature and content of this *bonum*.

In a case from Armagh (Ireland) judged *coram* Turnaturi on 14 March 1996[141], the first instance court established the grounds of nullity as follows: "Defective consent amounting to Total Simulation in the Petitioner. Inability to fulfil and assume the obligations of marriage in the Respondent"[142]. The first instance decision was negative on total simulation on the petitioner's part and affirmative on the respondent's part, that is, his "inability to assume and fulfil the essential obligations of marriage"[143]. The second instance court pronounced affirmatively on simulation ground and overturned the preceding affirmative ground on inability of the respondent for lack of consistency in evidence. Because the first instance negative decision was not appealed by the petitioner, the Rotal court decided to judge the case only on the ground of incapacity of the respondent to assume the essential obligations of marriage.

---

[139] Ibid.476: "Et sic idem incapax fuit nedum consortium totius vitae, sed et profundam amicalem relationem instaurare."

[140] "Attenta proinde gravitate ac antecedentia causae naturae psychicae, quae in viro magnum pondus attigit, concludendum est, uti etiam ex peritorum iudicio in actis bene fundato eruitur, conventum incapacem fuisse assumendi essentiales obligationes matrimoniales, praesertim *quae fundant bonum coniugum, elementum constitutivum matrimonii*, ad quod foedus iugale indole sua est ordinatum" (c. BRUNO, 19 July 1991, pp. 476-477; emphasis added). For a similar conclusion, see c. PALESTRO, 6 June 1991, in ME, 116 (1991), p. 378.

[141] See decision *c.* TURNATURI, 14 March 1996, in RRT *Dec.*, 88 (1996), pp. 234-256.

[142] Ibid., p. 235. It should be noted here that this case was introduced on 21 October 1976 before the ecclesiastical tribunal for a decision.

[143] Ibid.

In reference to the object of incapacity to assume, Turnaturi says that it "primarily concerns the impossibility of weaving together or establishing the interpersonal relationship that is truly matrimonial by its very nature ordered to the good of both spouses, or, if you wish, ordered primarily to a tolerable common life and juridically interwoven by its own obligations of justice. The canonical norm, however, relies on natural law because, there is no obligation to the impossible. [...]"[144]. Turnaturi considers *bonum coniugum* as an essential element of marriage, for he says that the capacity to assume conjugal obligations includes not only the three essential *bona* of marriage, namely fidelity, offspring and sacrament, but also the suitability (*habilitas*) to constitute the partnership of the whole of life ordered to the good of the spouses (*bonum coniugum*), "which is the essential element of marriage involving the interpersonal psychic capacity to establish with the partner at least a tolerable interpersonal relationship"[145]. Then Turnaturi quotes from a sentence by Stankiewicz in which the latter had identified the object of incapacity to assume the obligations of marriage. Turnaturi says:

> Also the essential obligations of marriage inherent to the good of the spouses can constitute" the object of this incapacity, "which substantially contribute to the establishment and perpetual sustenance of the communion of conjugal love between the spouses through mutual psycho-sexual integration ... Indeed, besides other essential rights and duties, as we are taught, 'there may be another essential right-obligation, which obliges the spouses to a specific communion and mutual solidarity which is not exhausted in their sexual dimension (*bonum fidei*) and in their generative mission (*bonum prolis*). The "suitable companionship" (*adiutorium simile sibi*) [Gen. 2, 18], which each spouse has the obligation to offer to the other and has the right to demand from the other, is not only a "companionship" (*adiutorium*) for the "remedy of concupiscence" and for the generation and education of children, but also the one directed to the well-being and perfection of the spouses themselves, taken in their totality, and not solely in their sexual and generative dimension'[146].

This observation derived from Navarrete, assumed as authoritative by the Rotal judges, seems to me the most appropriate manner of under-

---

[144] Ibid., p. 237.

[145] Ibid., p. 240.

[146] Ibid., pp. 240-241. Here the reference is to Urbano NAVARRETE, "Problemi sull'autonomia dei capi di nullità del matrimonio per difetto di consenso causato da perturbazioni della personalità," in *Problemi psichiche e consenso matrinoniale nel diritto canonico*, Roma, Officium Libri Catholici – Catholic Book Agnecy, 1976; sentence *c.* STANKIEWICZ, 21 June 1990, in RRT *Dec.*, 82 (1990), p. 525.

standing and defining the elements of the good of the spouses. It is the good of the total person – a being consisting of not only a body fitted with sexual drive but also a psycho-spiritual entity which aspires a much deeper interior personal perfection. It is the function of canonical doctrine and jurisprudence to determine the constitutive elements of this personal interior perfection of each spouse and of the spousal communion.

In this case, the respondent was diagnosed by the experts as suffering from affective immaturity, anxiety and narcissistic personality disorder. He was physically violent toward his wife, his sexual demands were excessive, and he was incapable of providing for the family because of his inconstancy in maintaining employment. The Rotal *turnus* concluded: "The respondent always presented himself "self-centered, mentally unstable and totally inadequate and incapable of facing up the responsibilities he had assumed"[147]. But no reference was made to *bonum coniugum* in the dispositive part of the sentence.

In a case from Olomouc (Ceská Republika) judged *coram* Bruno on 17 May 1996[148], the respondent woman was alleged to have been incapable of assuming the essential obligations of marriage because of serious psycho-affective immaturity. As he has done in the past, Bruno reiterates his view on the real content of *bonum coniugum* in his sentence. He says:

> The good of the spouses consists of assuming and fulfilling all obligations which make real the intimate union and integration of persons in offering to each other mutual help in the spiritual, material and social aspects so that a true conjugal life is established and lived out in peace and growth[149].

The decision of the Rotal *turnus* was affirmative on the ground of incapacity to assume the obligation of the good of the spouses (*bonum coniugum*). This is how Bruno expresses his assessment of the respondent's incapacity:

> The personality make up of the respondent, at first sight, appears to be sufficiently psychologically distorted. Clearly manifest are her serious psycho-affective immaturity, extreme dependency on both her mother and grandmother, depression, excessive self-love, inconstancy (irresponsibility) and an incapacity to live out a true partnership of conjugal life, that is, to

---

[147] *C.* TURNATURI, 14 March 1996, p. 256.

[148] See decision *c*. BRUNO, 17 May 1996, in RRT *Dec.*, 88 (1996), pp. 387-395.

[149] Ibid., 390: "Bonum enim coniugum amplectitur susceptionem et adimpletionem omnium obligationum quae realem reddunt intimam coniunctionem ac integrationem personarum in adiutorio sibi mutuo praestando in ordine spirituali, materiali et sociali ut vera coniugalis instauretur ac pacifice et progressive ducatur."

promote the good of the spouses to which marriage is by its very nature ordered[150].

The evidence clearly indicated that the respondent was seriously immature. She was not able to make decisions for herself. Her mother and grandmother made the decisions for her. She was constantly depressed, anxious and unsure of herself. The Rotal expert diagnosed her condition as "hysterical-depressive disturbances with psycho-affective immaturity and very little psychological autonomy in making decisions"[151]. After evaluating all evidence, including expert reports, Bruno concluded: "Consequently, we should conclude that the woman was totally unfit to establish a tolerable married life and to foster the *good of the spouses*, to which marriage is by its very nature ordered"[152]. Bruno does not indicate what elements or aspects of the *bonum coniugum* were denied to the petitioner or to the consortium totius vitae due to the psychological disorder of the respondent.

In a case from Jounieh (Lebanon) judged *coram* Jarawan on 24 July 1996[153], the Rotal expert reported that the respondent woman was suffering from serious paranoid personality disorder which became manifest only in married life and this "psycho-characterological" constitutional structure impeded her from realising "the dimension of the *bonum coniugum*." Jarawan does not identify the element(s) of the *bonum coniugum* which was affected by the paranoid personality disorder. It seems the experts had suggested that the respondent could not relate meaningfully to her spouse at the level of affect (emotions). The Rotal *turnus* made the expert's opinion its own and pronounced an affirmative decision on the respondent's incapacity to assume the essential obligation of *bonum coniugum* in accord with the norm of CCEO c. 818, 3°[154].

These Rotal sentences certainly demonstrate the fact that marriage cases can be judged on the ground of incapacity to assume the essential obligation of orienting the spousal relationship to the good of each

[150] Ibid., p. 392: "Personalitas Conventae in suo complexu, iam primo ictu oculi, psychologice sat distorta apparet; praedicatur illius gravis immaturitas psycho-affectiva, extrema dependentia tum a matre tum ab avia, depressio, immoderatus sui amor, levitas (irresponsabilitas) et incapacitas ducendi verum consortium vitae coniugalis, i.e., promovendi bonum coniugum ad quod matrimonium indole sua naturali ordinatur."

[151] Ibid., p. 394.

[152] Ibid., p. 395: "Proinde concludi debet mulierem minime idoneam fuisse ad vitam matrimonialem tolerabilem instaurandam et ad *bonum coniugum* promovendum, ad quod matrimonium natura sua ordinatur." (Emphasis added).

[153] See decision *c*. JARAWAN, 24 July 1996, in RRT *Dec.*, 88 (1996), pp. 544-565.

[154] Ibid., p. 565.

partner as a person, spouse and parent, and to the good of the total spousal relationship which is created by the irrevocable personal consent of the parties. Not all judges attempt to delineate the essential specifics of *bonum coniugum* and rather stay at the level of the general principle. For example, one could try to identify what aspect of the personal well being is affected by a particular disorder in a concrete case. In some cases it might be the physical well being, in others it could be emotional, sexual, moral, spiritual, or material well being of the spouse. Such an approach, of course, would call for a deeper study of the human personality and the effects mental disorders could have on a person's capacity for conjugal interpersonal relationship, the very core of spousal and parental life.

The Rotal sentences reviewed here make no reference to any cultural aspects of the concrete cases. Therefore, it is difficult to point out any specific cultural influences that might have contributed to the incapacity to assume the essential obligations flowing from *bonum coniugum*. But one thing seems clear in all these sentences, that is, *bonum coniugum* is now being clearly regarded as the object of incapacity mentioned in c. 1095 (CCEO c. 818).

CONCLUSION

The Second Vatican Council in its dogmatic constitution, *Lumen gentium* 17, said: "The effect of her work is that whatever good is found sown in the minds and hearts of people or in the rites and customs of peoples, these not only are preserved from destruction, but are purified, raised up, and perfected for the glory of God ..."[155]. This constitutes the Church's fundamental teaching on the relationship between its divine mission and the cultures of the world. According to the Church's admission, culture represents a unique ritual and customary heritage cherished by the people in their minds and hearts, that is to say, a heritage deeply rooted in their concrete lives. The Church accepts and respects what is good in people's cultures. For this reason, the council reminds us in *GS* 59 that we should respect the mode of living of human beings in society: "Culture, since it flows from man's rational and social nature, has continual need of rightful freedom ... Quite rightly it demands respect and enjoys a certain inviolability, provided, of course, that the rights of the

---

[155] See FLANNERY I, pp. 368-369.

individual and the community, both particular and universal, are safe-guarded within the limits of the common good"[156].

The Rotal Auditor, B. De Lanversin, has incorporated these insights of the council into one of his recent sentences while dealing with a marriage case which originated in Calcutta (India)[157]. Although the sentence itself has no reference to *bonum coniugum* as such, the emphasis on the importance of culture vis-à-vis marriage is quite evident.

The marriage under consideration was arranged according to the local custom by the parents of the parties. De Lanversin refers to statements from conciliar discussions to emphasise how some fathers of the council, particularly those coming from Africa and Asia, insisted on respecting the cultural values pertaining to marriage. For example, the Archbishop of Djakarta (Indonesia) presented the following observation on the importance of considering cultural influences on the nature of marriage: "... outside the western culture, marriage is generally not contracted through the mutual love of the parties, who often hardly know each other, but through the will of their parents or clan. The covenant, therefore, is not the result of love. Rather mutual love is considered as the fruit of marriage which gradually matures"[158]. In a later intervention, the same Archbishop, representing the African and Asian prelates, again returned to the theme saying: "... I pleaded for your consideration in regard to the forms of marriage, which are found in regions of non-western culture ... In our regions and in some others, there still prevails the form of marriage in which it is not the personal love between the husband and wife but the intention to establish a family in society that impels them to marry. The very first thing intended in marriage is the establishment of a family so that the family lineage (clan) may be perpetuated. And it is precisely this intention which results in true love or at least mutual and stable trust between the husband and the wife"[159]. One can clearly see the importance of these statements for local jurisprudence. The same principles are applicable also to western cultures which are witnessing revolutionary changes in social, religious and moral values which inevitably affect the way people perceive those values and make choices touching their lives.

---

[156] *GS* 59; FLANNERY I, p. 963.
[157] Decision *c*. DE LANVERSIN, 27 June 1997 (Calcutta, India), Prot. No. 16.901 (unpublished).
[158] *Acta synodalia,* vol. III, pars VIII, p. 669.
[159] Ibid., vol. IV, pars III, p. 69.

Whether or not the new codes have given any serious consideration to these pleas could constitute interesting matter for further research, but the fact remains that any interpretation of the present legislation on marriage absolutely cannot overlook the importance of these interventions. In other words, as jurists concerned with the spiritual well being of Christ's faithful, we cannot prescind from cultural contexts while interpreting and applying the law, especially the law which deals with marriage and family.

In his Rotal allocution of 21 January 1999, John Paul II said: "Everyone knows the contribution which the jurisprudence of your Tribunal has made to our knowledge of the institution of marriage by offering a very sound doctrinal reference-point for other ecclesiastical tribunals [...] This has made it possible to bring into ever better focus the essential content of marriage on the basis of a more *adequate knowledge* of the *human person*"[160].

This statement of the Holy Father has a very important point for our consideration. In it the Holy Father implies that the extent of knowledge we can have of the content of marriage would be in proportion to the knowledge we have of the human person. Therefore, the deeper our knowledge of the *human person* the deeper will be our knowledge of the nature and content of marriage. It is reasonable to argue, therefore, that the determination of the nature and content of *bonum coniugum* would depend to a large extent on the knowledge we have of the human person incarnate in a specific and concrete culture. The essential good of this person would depend on what that person **is** within the context of a particular culture.

The elements of the *bonum coniugum*, the realisation or failure of realisation of those elements in the concrete life of the couple, would depend largely on the nature and forces of each culture which define the way of life for its people. This does not imply that everything should be relativised for the sake of adopting the notion of marriage and its elements to a particular culture. No, the institutional nature of marriage as the church teaches is derived from natural law and revelation, and therefore, it is universally applicable to all of humanity. What it does imply, however, is the fact that the life of people, whether they be individuals or groups, is invariably moulded and shaped by the concrete cultural

---

[160] JOHN PAUL II, Allocution to the Roman Rota, 21 January 1999, in *L'Osservatore romano*, Weekly English language edition, 10 February 1999, p. 3. Emphasis added.

forces, and we cannot dismiss them as irrelevant to our discussion on the nature and elements of *bonum coniugum*.

At present both law and jurisprudence acknowledge that *bonum coniugum* is an institutional end of marriage. And as an intrinsic end, that is, one that flows from the very nature of marriage, it becomes a constitutive element of the object of matrimonial consent. Therefore, the ordering of marriage covenant or marriage itself to *bonum coniugum* thus turns into a constitutive element of the object of consent. Specific rights and obligations arise from this element. Once we admit this principle, it is natural to assume that this element can be excluded from consent either by a deliberate act of will or by an incapacity rooted in the personality of the contractant(s).

As this study demonstrates, the most difficult problem with which both scholars and practitioners are wrestling today concerns the content of the *bonum coniugum*. What is the content of this *bonum coniugum*? Theories and suggestions on this question abound in canonical literature. We believe that valid and fruitful analysis of the *bonum coniugum* is possible only when the true nature of the well being of each spouse as a *human person* is determined. As John Paul II has clearly stated, this goal could be achieved only when we have a true anthropological understanding of the human person within the context of a particular culture which defines his/her personal and cultural identity.

A person's decision to marry is always made within the concrete context of his/her culture, whether western or eastern, northern or southern. That decision is formed in accord with the cultural mores. For example, in the western culture a person's decision to marry is made without any intervention from family or other significant persons. It is the consent of the parties alone that is the efficient cause of marriage. Therefore, when c. 1057 (CCEO c. 817, §1) says that consent is an act of the will by which a man and a woman "mutually give and accept each other" (*"sese mutuo tradunt et accipiunt"*), it means for a westerner only a personal consent involving strictly a personal self-donation. But for a person in Africa or Asia, the *"sese"* of the canon would necessarily involve, besides personal consent and self-donation, not only the consent of parents or of the tribal elder(s) but also the *bonding* of their families. In other words, in African or Asian cultures, the expression *"sese"* of the canon would constitute a symbol of gifting not only of the spouses but also of their respective families. Similarly, while the *bonum coniugum* in general means within the western cultures the good of each spouse as a person and of the spouses together, it has a very different connotation in an African or Asian culture. In the latter, the good of the spouses is necessarily interwoven with the good of the families and/or of the clan/tribe.

The above concluding observations highlight the complexity of the issues involved and emphasise the need to interpret canonical principles in light of cultural forces which are likely to shape the nature and content of *bonum coniugum* within the context of a socio-culturally distinct people. It seems obvious from this study that experts in canon law have much work to do in determining, in a scientific manner, the more specific juridic aspects of the *bonum coniugum* from both doctrinal and cultural perspectives.

PERSONALIA

AUGUSTINE MENDONÇA, born in 1941, was ordained to the presbyterate for the diocese of Mangalore, India, on 3 December 1966. He is presently a priest of the diocese of Montego Bay, Jamaica, WI. University studies: B.A. (Psychology), Karnataka University, Dharward, India, 1970; Master's Degree in Clinical Psychology, University of Ottawa, ON, 1976; M.A. (Religion and Medical Care), George Washington University, Washington, DC, 1977; J.C.L., Saint Paul University, Ottawa, ON; M.C.L., University of Ottawa, ON, 1979; Diploma in Canonical Jurisprudence, Pontifical Gregorian University, Rome, 1980; Ph.D. (CL), University of Ottawa, and J.C.D., Saint Paul University, Ottawa, 1982; M.A. (Theol.), 2000, and S.T.L. 2001, "Angelicum" University, Rome. He is a full professor in the Faculty of Canon Law, Saint Paul University, Ottawa. Canada. He has written extensively in several international canonical journals on different substantive aspects of marriage consent and justice and equity as well as on a variety of procedural issues.

JIŘI RAJMUND TRETERA was born in Prague (Czech Republic) in 1940. He studied law and international law (first graduation, 1962; JUDr., 1967) at the Faculty of Law, Charles University. As a Christian, he could not teach at any school, and became a business lawyer. He studied theology at the clandestine General Study of the Dominicans in Prague from 1980, and he started to teach canon law at the same institute from 1984. He secretly joined the Dominican Order (1987). After the revolution of 1989, he started to live in St. Giles' Priory in Prague. He was ordained a priest (1991). Since 1990, he gives lectures in canon law, state ecclesiastical law and legal history at the Faculty of Law, Charles University. He has been a Docent Professor of those subjects since his habilitation in 1993. He is a member of the *Consociatio Internationalis Studio Iuris Canonici Promovendo*, an associate member of the *Centre for Law and Religion*, Cardiff. He participated in activies of the *European Consortium for Church and State Research*. He is a president of the Church Law Society, Prague. J. R. Tretera published four books and more than 40 articles in canon law, state ecclesiastical law, legal history. He is an editor of the Church Law Review and a member of the editorial staff of the *Acta Universitatis Carolinae – Iuridica*.

Rik Torfs was born in Turnhout (Belgium) in 1956. He studied law (lic. iur., 1979; lic. not., 1980) and canon law (J.C.D., 1987) at the Katholieke Universiteit Leuven. After one year of teaching at Utrecht University (The Netherlands), he became professor at the Faculty of Canon Law (K.U. Leuven) in 1988. He is dean of the Faculty of Canon Law since 1993 and visiting professor at the University of Stellenbosch (South Africa) since 2000. He is a member of the Board of Directors of the *European Consortium for State-Church Research*. R. Torfs published eight books and more than 200 articles on canon law, law, church and state relationships. He is editor of the *European Journal for Church and State Research*.

PUBLICATIES / PUBLICATIONS
MSGR. W. ONCLIN CHAIR

Editor Rik TORFS

Canon Law and Marriage. Monsignor W. Onclin Chair 1995, **Leuven, Peeters, 1995, 36 p.**

R. TORFS, *The Faculty of Canon Law of K.U. Leuven in 1995*, 5-9.
C. BURKE, *Renewal, Personalism and Law*, 11-21.
R.G.W. HUYSMANS, *Enforcement and Deregulation in Canon Law*, 23-36.

A Swing of the Pendulum. Canon Law in Modern Society. Monsignor W. Onclin Chair 1996, **Leuven, Peeters, 1996, 64 p.**

R. TORFS, *Une messe est possible. Over de nabijheid van Kerk en geloof*, 7-11.
R. TORFS, *'Une messe est possible'. A Challenge for Canon Law*, 13-17.
J.M. SERRANO RUIZ, *Acerca del carácter personal del matrimonio: digresiones y retornos*, 19-31.
J.M. SERRANO RUIZ, *The Personal Character of Marriage. A Swing of the Pendulum*, 33-45.
F.G. MORRISEY, *Catholic Identity of Healthcare Institutions in a Time of Change*, 47-64.

In Diversitate Unitas. Monsignor W. Onclin Chair 1997, **Leuven, Peeters, 1997, 72 p.**

R. TORFS, *Pro Pontifice et Rege*, 7-13.
R. TORFS, *Pro Pontifice et Rege*, 15-22.
H. PREE, *The Divine and the Human of the Ius Divinum*, 23-41.
J.H. PROVOST, *Temporary Replacements or New Forms of Ministry: Lay Persons with Pastoral Care of Parishes*, 43-70.

Bridging Past and Future. Monsignor W. Onclin Revisited. Monsignor W. Onclin Chair 1998, **Leuven, Peeters, 1998, 87 p.**

P. CARD. LAGHI, *Message*, 7-9.
R. TORFS, *Kerkelijk recht in de branding. Terug naar monseigneur W. Onclin*, 11-20.
R. TORFS, *Canon Law in the Balance. Monsignor W. Onclin Revisited*, 21-31.

L. ÖRSY, *In the Service of the Holy Spirit: the Ecclesial Vocation of the Canon Lawyers*, 33-53.
P. COERTZEN, *Protection of Rights in the Church. A Reformed Perspective*, 55-87.

Church and State. Changing Paradigms. Monsignor W. Onclin Chair 1999, Leuven, Peeters, 1999, 72 p.

R. TORFS, *Crisis in het kerkelijk recht*, 7-17.
R. TORFS, *Crisis in Canon Law*, 19-29.
C. MIGLIORE, *Ways and Means of the International Activity of the Holy See*, 31-42.
J.E. WOOD, JR., *The Role of Religion in the Advancement of Religious Human Rights*, 43-69.

Canon Law and Realism. Monsignor W. Onclin Chair 2000, Leuven, Peeters, 2000, 92 p.

R. TORFS, *De advocaat in de kerk, of de avonturen van een vreemdeling in het paradijs*, 7-28.
R. TORFS, *The Advocate in the Church. Source of Conflict or Conflict Solver*, 29-49.
J.P. BEAL, *At the Crossroads of Two Laws. Some Reflections on the Influence of Secular Law on the Church's Response to Clergy Sexual Abuse in the United States*, 51-74.
CH.K. PAPASTATHIS, *Unity Among the Orthodox Churches. From the Theological Approach to the Historical Realities*, 75-88.

Canon Law Between Interpretation and Imagination. Monsignor W. Onclin Chair 2001, Leuven, Peeters, 2001, 88 p.

J. CORIDEN, *Necessary Canonical Reform: Urgent Issues for the Future*, 7-25.
R. PAGÉ, *Full Time Lay Pastoral Ministers and Diocesan Governance*, 27-40.
R. TORFS, *Kerkelijke rechtbanken* secundum *en* praeter legem, 41-61.
R. TORFS, *Church Tribunals* secundum *and* praeter legem, 63-84.